Spik o the Place

Norman Harper

SPIK O THE PLACE

·

Foreword by Robbie Shepherd

·

Illustrated by Charles Hynes

CANONGATE

First published in Great Britain in 1998 by
Canongate Books Ltd
14 High Street
Edinburgh EH1 1TE

10 9 8 7 6 5 4 3 2 1

ISBN 0 86241 834 8

British Library Cataloguing-in-Publication Data
A catalogue record for this volume is available
on request.

Typeset by Palimpsest Book Production Limited
Polmont, Stirlingshire
Printed and bound by Caledonian International, Bishopbriggs

Foreword

As I gaed doon by Memsie
I heard an aul man speir
'Faur's the bonnie dialect
'That aince wis spoken here?'
TEMPORA MUTANTUR
J. C. Milne

In that most descriptive poem, John C. Milne looked back to an earlier part of the 20th century, recalling a way of life he saw slipping away from the Buchan of his youth, with its independent, some say dour, rural life.

The birn o barfit bairnies. The steady fine-gyaun pairie.
The brose caup an the skimmer. The grauvit and the dickie.

If only those who planned our educational needs had followed the example of J. C., the bonnie, birlin words would never have been allowed to gather dust in the bookshelves of our schools.

In common with others of my generation, I had the North-east spik drummed out of me as being somewhat vulgar, and surely not a tongue if you had ambitions to get on in the world.

Sic claivers. I could name many who became major figures in their own sphere, home and abroad, without ever losing the mither tongue. Charles Murray, for instance, left Donside at the tail end of the last century to carve out a fine career in South Africa, but he never forgot his roots, and his thoughts on his homeland were penned so graphically in the poems he sent back.

Drift oxter-deep haps Bennachie

A far cry for the exile in the searing heat to the longing in the heart to be with the folks and climate that were so natural to him.

v

Drift oxter-deep haps Bennachie. What a descriptive phrase and, like most of Murray's thoughts, it loses everything in translation. It's rooted in the North-east alone.

So what about today, then? Well, it's still here; bonnie words sometimes, and roch words, but identifying indelibly the character and the way of life in the North-east.

I am often confronted with the dismissive remark that 'naebody spiks lik that noo', but if I were to put a tape-recorder and microphone in front of the utterer, he would find that that was exactly how he was saying it.

Here, in *Spik o the Place*, we are greatly indebted to Norman Harper for bringing into focus the rich vernacular of today, from town and country, with a clever combination of words, phrases and down-to-earth examples. Our eyes hover on a particular word and a whole episode in our memories comes to the fore. Take the gentle sympathy on the loss of a dear one whose last days had been spent in much suffering: *He's awa fae't aa noo.*

Of course, the chapters wouldn't be complete without the *claik ower the gairden wa* with the neighbours being *taen throwe haun.* There's the *bidey-in* with a *tongue that wid clip cloots* and her next door with the *hudderie heid* like *cattie's sookins.*

Enough of that. You'll come on your own favourite, I'm sure; words and phrases that are difficult to translate but then, translation is not the object of this book.

Norman reminds us of the whole tapestry of our North-east corner where the *Spik o the Place* forms such an integral part.

As Ian Middleton, one of our current poets, puts it:

> *Tho nations hae each got their ain mode o speech*
> *Some weel kent an ithers unsung*
> *They wid better the breed usin certified seed*
> *Lik the Doric, wir ain mither tongue.*

Robbie Shepherd
September 1998

Introduction

First, a word about what this book is not. It is not a dictionary of Doric. Many people who are devoted to that form of Scots spoken in North-east Scotland have undertaken the phenomenal task of recording the language of years long gone and preserving words and phrases which speak of lives as they were lived in conditions we can barely imagine now. It is important that the old vocabularies of fishers and farmers are preserved and revered and I commend these works to you.

In the three years that Canongate Books have been at me to write *Spik o the Place*, the brief has never wavered: they wanted a collection of the vernacular that is in current use in the North-east of Scotland. The theory is that it is easier to preserve something which is still vibrant and quick.

This broth of Doric, slang and strangulated English is the unabashed hybrid which has resulted. It is the product of the memories and speech of many dozens of friends and acquaintances. It is also the product of spending more than a year sitting in cafés and tearooms, standing in supermarkets and post-office queues, and generally eavesdropping shamelessly when I know perfectly well that I shouldn't have been doing any such thing.

The results have come from all age groups. The youngest contributor to my notes was just eight years old. The oldest that I know of was 95. That has given me a good spread of age, interest and background to make the collection more authentic.

I have three requests. You have to be born and brought up in the North-east to know how marked is the cultural and linguistic difference between Aberdeen city and the rural part of the region. I hope that the Toonsers will indulge the Teuchters and vice versa throughout the book. Enjoy each other's words and sayings, even if they might not be familiar to you.

Secondly, the language changes minutely from village to village and glen to glen, with the effect that the dialect spoken in Buchan is different from that spoken in Banffshire, which is different from Donside's, which is different from Deeside's, which differs from Kincardine's, and so on and so on. If your own area's words are spelled differently, or your phrases are not quite the same, trust me that the version you read here is the authentic version to someone. I know yours will be just as good, and I'd like to hear about them.

Thirdly, I hope those of you who are of delicate sensibilities and who cock your crannie at fly-cup time will excuse me some of the riper sayings and words. I could have left them out, but that would have denied the colour and vigour of everyday speech in this part of the country, and the book wouldn't have been the same without them. Besides, you don't really expect me to believe that you're surprised that the North-east has a curious interest in bodily functions and in the myriad effects of alcohol.

Anyway, here it is. More than 1,000 examples of language which is still in daily use and which, like all the best descriptive Doric and dialect, tell it het and rikkin.

Norman Harper
October, 1998

Acknowledgements

You don't produce a book as complicated as this without a great deal of help and I must thank many people. First, Neville Moir, Hugh Andrew and the team at Canongate Books for refusing repeatedly over three years to listen to my pleas of exhaustion; my agent, Alison Reid, who took a curious delight in hearing that I was working until 3 a.m. many mornings; Robbie Shepherd, whose devotion to Doric is second to none, and who kindly wrote the foreword and cast an eye over the finished manuscript; the contributors who knowingly jotted down words and phrases of their own:

Isobel Balfour	Frances and John Duncan
Norman Duncan	Tommy Forsyth
Rena and Ron Gaiter	Alice Kemp
Ruaridh McWhirr	Caroline Massie
Claire Massie	Ruth Nicol
Chrissabel Reid	Iris Robertson
Violet Taylor	Anne Thomson
Dorothy Watson	My wife, Alison
	and my parents

as well as the many hundreds of unwitting 'contributors' to whom I owe profound apologies for lugging into your conversations. I hope I am forgiven.

This book is dedicated to my Aunt Ruth and Aunt Vitie.

A

Aa dirt or aa butter
All dirt or all butter. Doric in a philosophical mood, meaning there's never a happy medium; it's always all good fortune or all disaster. This phrase is used especially by self-employed tradesmen lamenting the seasonal nature of their businesses.

Aa in ae shop
All in one shop. Any child given pocket money or any gift of money, however small, is encouraged not to spend it 'aa in ae shop'. You might take this as an encouragement to thrift, but these days it's said more in jest, especially if the gift is £1 or less, which, given the North-east, is highly likely.

1

Aa on ae plate

Describing an insubstantial reward. These days, said most often of someone who works above and beyond the call for an ungrateful or exploitative employer. 'Johnnie works twelve oors a day, sax days a wikk, and disna get nae overtime. He'll maybe get his reward, bit it'll be aa on ae plate.'

Aa ower the back

Completely out of control. An Aberdonian expression from the 1930s, when many families stayed in tenements and habitually turfed the children out to play in the back close. In naturally high spirits, the children would race across every square inch of the close, shouting and squealing, seemingly deranged with excitement. Hence, it's a suitable description of any display of uncommonly high spirits verging on complete stupidity. 'Did ye see the clowns on the TV last nicht? Wis thon nae aa ower the back?'

Ace o picks

Ace of spades. Can refer to the playing card, but heard most often when describing something which is black or profoundly dirty. 'Awa up the stairs and wash yer face. Ye're as black as the ace o picks.'

Adee

Wrong or *ado.* A word heard very rarely on its own; more often as part of the friendly query: 'Fit's adee?', meaning 'What's wrong?'

Aenoo

Just now. 'Far are ye gaun aenoo?'

Affa

Very or *terribly.* All-purpose Doric word which is used to apply emphasis. No one is ill in the North-east; we are 'affa nae weel'. There are no thunderstorms; we have 'an affa day o rain'. We don't break the speed limit; we 'ging at an affa lick'. You get the idea.

Ace o picks

Ale

Any soft fizzy drink. 'Mam, can I hae a drink o ale?' 'Awa doon til the shoppie for a bottle o ale.' Also known as Dazzle in some parts of Banffshire and Buchan, after the North-east's own version of cola. Most of those who tried Dazzle swore it was immeasurably superior to the ubiquitous American stuff. Must never be confused with the English alcoholic 'ale'. It's an easy mistake, made most notably by a Lanarkshire-born teacher arriving to start his first day's work at Inverurie Academy in the 1970s. He overheard two second-year boys agreeing to go downtown at break time to buy themselves a bottle of ale. On reporting them to the headmaster, he was let down suitably gently.

Aneth the bed

Safe keeping. Whether or not the stash is kept below the bed, this phrase describes any secret hidey-hole, which might range from the top of a wardrobe to the back of the airing cupboard. They are all 'aneth the bed'. 'Far hiv ye hidden the loon's Christmas present?' 'Aneth the bed.' It stems from older Scots' suspicion of banks which even now has many keeping their funds 'in a tinnie aneth the bed'.

Ask for

To inquire after someone's health. 'Tell yer dad I wis askin for him.' Doric-speakers would use the word 'speirin' instead of 'askin'.

At blaiks aa

That beats everything. 'So yer wife's expectin saxtuplets, Ernie. Weel, weel, 'at blaiks aa.'

Aul claes and porritch

Old clothes and porridge. At the end of a holiday, when all the spending money has gone, one observes ruefully that one must return to the daily grind. 'Back til the work the morn. Back tae aul claes and porritch.'

Austrian blinds
A ruched arrangement of curtains for living-room windows. Almost endemically popular throughout the North-east in the 1980s, but now regarded almost universally as naff in the extreme.

Awa fae't aa
Away from it all. Dead, in other words. 'That's him awa fae't aa noo.' If the death is thought to have been a merciful release, someone will observe philosophically: 'He's better aff awa.'

Awa ye go
I don't believe you. 'Yer mither's a size twelve? Awa ye go.' As an alternative, you might try: 'Awa and burst.'

Ay-ay
A greeting used more as an acknowledgment in passing, no reply expected. 'Ay-ay, Wullie. Fine day.'

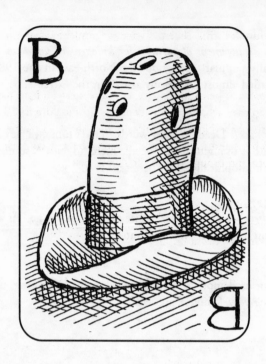

B

Ba Up
No literal translation, but short for the Aberdonian expression 'Ba up on the slates', meaning something which has gone badly wrong. 'I said I needed a plumber here yesterday morning. Now I'm knee-deep in water. What happened?' 'Sorry, sir, the hale office his been ba up since the wikkend.' Derives from a children's backyard kickabout game. If the ball got stuck on a roof and couldn't be retrieved, the game came to an abrupt end and everyone had to shuffle home. The 'ba' had gone 'up on the slates'.

Bachles
Shoes beyond repair. The CH is pronounced as in Loch. 'I peyed

thirty poun for this sheen. Twice on and that's them bachles already.'

Baffies
House slippers. 'There's nithing sae comfortin efter a hard day's wark as a soak in the bath, pittin on yer goon and shochlin in yer baffies.' Some parts of the North-east know baffies as safties. Safties are also sandwich buns and stupid people. It can all be very confusing unless you're born and brought up in the North-east.

Bakin
The act of cooking pastries and cakes in the home, but also the collective noun for anything thus produced. 'Come awa in for a fly cup, Gertie. I've nae lang finished a bakin.'

Bandit
Cowboy tradesman. 'That plumber crackit oor Tibbie's sink and charged her twa hunder poun. He's jist a bandit.'

Banffie
The Banffshire Journal. Weekly newspaper covering the old county, which is still required reading in that part of the North-east. Now part of a larger weekly-paper group. 'I'll hae a packet o Senior Service, a quarter o pan drops and ma Banffie.'

Bannocks
Large thin pancakes (as opposed to girdle scones or drop scones). Bannocks are also double chins, expressed most clearly in the tale in which a woman wonders if her husband finds her less attractive because she has turned so fat. 'Nivver a fat,' he says, 'though there's whiles I think ye're keekin at me ower a pile o bannocks.' Bannocks can also be oatcakes in some parts of the North-east.

Bap-face
One whose complexion is alarmingly pale. 'What a bap-face Wullie hid fin he cam oot o Forsterhill.' There is also a school of thought that a bap face is a *soft, pudgy and stupid-looking face.* Naturally, there are no such things in North-east Scotland.

Bandit

Bap feet
Flat-footed. 'Oor Ed wisna in the Army durin the waar. They widna tak him for his bap feet.'

Bap poodin
Bread-and-butter pudding, to anyone else.

Bappit
Collided. 'I wis mindin ma ain business at the traffic-lichts and some gype bappit intae the back o me.'

Bare nakit
Starkers. 'There's far ower mony bare-nakit wifies on the TV nooadays. Gie's back Minnie Caldwell, I say.'

Barkit
Excessively dirty. 'Foo lang hiv ye been weerin that sark, Jim? Yer collar's barkit.'

Bate
Defeated. 'Their centre-half jinkit left, jinkit richt and syne haimmered it in. That wis them bate.'

Beamer
Blush. 'I catched them canoodlin at the back o the bike sheds and she took a richt beamer.'

Beens
Bones, not the tinned vegetable. Hence: 'I'm affa troubled wi ma beens,' is a sign of rheumatism, not gastric embarrassment.

Beardie
A peculiar expression of affection between a North-east father and his children, possible only when he is unshaven. The child is grabbed and the father's face is rubbed vigorously along the child's cheek. When concluded, the father laughs uproariously and the

9

child goes in search of a bucket of ice, a tub of calamine lotion and a shoulder upon which to cry. Affection is apparently a difficult concept for North-east fathers. Hence: 'Why have you come to school with your head swathed in bandages, Alfred?' 'Got a beardie fae ma dad last nicht, miss. He loves me really.'

Beerial
Interment. 'Will we see ye at the beerial, Mina?' 'Na, na, I'll jist ging til the kirk service and then hame. Beerials is nae for weemin.'

Bennachie bap
Sweet bun worked into a pronounced conical peak and sprinkled with that form of confectioner's sugar which resembles small hailstones. Very popular until the late 1960s, but now made by only a very few family-owned bakeries. Bennachie is Central Aberdeenshire's most prominent and most celebrated hill. 'Sees a half-dizzen o yer Bennachie baps.'

Berrens
Aberdeen word for children. 'Ma man and me dinna bother muckle wi Christmas. Well, Christmas is for the berrens.'

The Berries
Soft-fruit picking. In the late summer school holidays, children who had exasperated their parents or who needed to earn extra pocket-money would be sent out to soft-fruit farms to pick strawberries or, more usually, rasps. These efforts were paid by weight, and the ploys dreamed up by some of the less scrupulous pickers to increase a punnet's weight would put anyone off shop-bought jam for life. Going to The Berries has become less common now that Pick Your Own businesses have expanded and become more popular.

Better days
The traditional answer to the question: 'Fit are you waitin for?'

Bick
A bitch. Used of canines, of course, but also of humans. In the

human context, it is rarely derogatory or uttered in anger. It is used most often as a term of affection and sympathy directed at an unmarried mother, as in: 'Ach, weel. A bick's aye the better o a pup.' (A bitch is always better to have had a pup.)

Bicyclin sark
Sunday-best shirt. The phrase is still used widely and derives from the days when farm servants would dress up to go out on a day off and the only transport available was the bicycle.

Bide
Live in. 'I bide at New Pitsligo.' **Bide** is not a synonym for **come fae**. One bides wherever one happens to be living at any given moment. One **comes fae** the place where one was brought up. The distinction is lost on many. 'I bide at New Pitsligo, bit I come fae Cruden Bay.'

Bidey-in
One who co-habits. 'Erchie says he mairriet her in South Africa, bit I hinna seen a ring. I doot she's jist a bidey-in.'

Bigsy
Snobbish. Used more often of women than men, hence: 'Mina's that bigsy, she thinks she farts Chanel Number Five.'

Biled dry
Said of someone who is past being merely exhausted and is near to collapse, either through hard labour or hard liquor. 'Awa hame tae yer bed, min. Ye're biled dry.'

Bilin
Any pot of vegetables which has been cooked, but said usually of potatoes. 'Come roon for yer denner, Isa. I've a bilin o new tatties and butter.'

Birdie's maet
Birdfood. The little crusty lumps which must be brushed from the

eyelashes and corners of the eyes after a night's sleep. 'Awa and wash yer face again, Donald. Yer een's still cakit wi birdie's maet.'

Bitta stuff
An exceptionally pulchritudinous young woman. 'Weel, Dode, that wis a richt bitta stuff ye left the dunce wi last nicht. Nae een o yer usual growlers.'

Blaa
A boaster or windbag. 'Davie's cousin's hame fae America. We've heard aboot his big cars and his big hoose and his sweemin-pool and his fittit kitchen. What a blaa.' An older North-easter would dismiss such a person as **'a bleeter o win'** '.

Blaad
To spoil or damage. Illustrated best by a story which John Duff of Braemar once told Robbie Shepherd and me about the young lad turning up at a home in Braemar to take the daughter of the house to a dance. Her father bade them farewell and, as the young couple were walking down the garden path, advised the boy: 'Noo dinna blaad the lassie.'

Black affrontit
Profoundly embarrassed. The 'black' alludes to the blush on the victim's face, which was supposedly so red that it turned purple, then almost black. 'Foo wis I tae ken she wis stannin ahen me aa the time? I wis black affrontit.'

Black Tam
A habitual funeral-goer. Even now, in small villages throughout northern Scotland, there are older residents who turn out to pay their respects whether they knew the deceased or not. This is regarded as a community duty, although some younger citizens are known to find it morbid. Mistakenly, the younger ones believe that Black Tams regard a funeral as an outing. The name comes from the mourning garb: a heavy black coat, black shoes

polished almost to extinction and, until very recently, a bowler hat. 'Davie's terrible bored wi retirement. I can see him turnin intil a Black Tam.'

Blaik
Shoe polish or dubbin. Irrespective of the nugget's colour, it is always referred to as blaik, hence: 'Grocer, hiv ye a tinnie o broon blaik?'

Blaik amon treacle
A black person in treacle. From the days when the North-east was less politically correct, this described absolute and unsurpassable happiness. 'Fin I wis your age, I jist got an aeple and an orange for ma birthday and I wis as happy as a blaik amon treacle.' Note that treacle is pronounced in the North-east as 'traikle'.

Bleezin
Drunk. 'He wis that bleezin last nicht they took him hame in a bucket.' Or: 'He spent sae muckle o his life bleezin that they canna hae the funeral at the Crem, for it wid tak a wikk tae pit oot the fire.'

Bleish
Sudden profusion, but used mostly of rainstorms. 'That's the last time I ging oot athoot a brolly. I wis catched in a bleish o rain.' Or: 'Isn't that bleish o poppies richt bonnie?'

Blin drift
A blizzard so fierce that visibility is down to zero. 'Ye canna leave noo, John. It's blin drift oot there.'

Blin lump
Pimple or boil at the sore stage just before it has begun to show and erupt. 'I canna sit doon, thanks aa the same. I've a blin lump.'

Blink afore a drink
That peculiar watery sun one gets shortly before a shower of rain during a North-east autumn. 'Fit's the weather deein?' 'Och, a blink afore a drink.'

Bloomers
A puff-pastry biscuit as big as the palm of a woman's hand. The item is smeared with sweet yellow or pink icing and is shaped like a pair of bloomers hanging on a washing-line. 'Fit will we hae wi wir fly cup, Ina?' 'Oh, they dee affa tasty bloomers in this caffy.' 'I'll hae a Kit-Kat if it's a' the same tae yersel.' See also **Coo's fit**.

Bondie
Bonfire. 'That's the mannie next door put up anither bondie and ma washin's aa smokit.'

Bonnie washin
The highest praise any North-east housewife can bestow on another. On washdays, a conscientious housewife fills the line with pristine and sparkling garments, which are ranked in order of size, colour and purpose. 'Say fit ye like aboot Elsie; she pits oot a bonnie washin.' One can also 'keep a bonnie hoose', 'dee a bonnie bakin' and 'clean a bonnie step'.

Bosie
A voluptuous embrace. Used most often to comfort distressed children. 'Skinned yer knees, ma we lamb? Come ower here for a bosie.' Derives from 'bosom', and the word can also be used of the female anatomy in the same context. 'Skinned yer knees? Come intae ma bosie and that'll mak it better.'

Bothyin
Any man looking after himself temporarily at home while his wife or girlfriend is working, holidaying, visiting relatives or otherwise detained away from base is said to be bothyin. Derives from the days when farmworkers looked after themselves in the farm bothy. 'Yer hoose is an affa sotter, Alick.' 'I'm bothyin aenoo. The wife's awa tae Dunbar for the wikkend. Are ye for a biled egg and soup?'

Braakfist
Literally 'breakfast', but also someone who has no dress sense. Derived

14

presumably from 'a dog's breakfast'. 'Check Rab ower at the bus stop. Fit a braakfist.'

Bradie
North-east version of the Forfar bridie. The recipe is pretty much the same – a pastry parcel filled with mince – except that the North-east version is a little smaller.

Bree
Any liquid pressed out of a solid. Thus, the whey which drips out of a cheesecloth is bree; the liquid screwed from wet socks after a day's hillwalking is bree, and the water left behind after any pan of vegetables is cooked is bree. The liquid content of a midden or a byre is **sharn bree**. To drain the cooking water from a pan of vegetables turns bree into a verb, as in: 'Claire, awa and bree the tatties.' What a multipurpose word.

Bree the tatties
Urinate. 'Weel, gentlemen, if ye'll excuse me for a mintie, I'll awa and bree the tatties.'

Breether
Nothing to do with a short rest; this is the Banffshire word for brother. 'Ma breether's got a rare new job wi the Watter Boord.'

The Breider
An establishment in old Harriet Street, Aberdeen, where bakery goods which were no longer fresh were sold at knockdown prices. Demolished when the Bon-Accord Centre shopping mall was erected in the late 1980s. The word can also be used of anything or anyone that is looking decidedly second-hand. 'Erchie wis clubbin til five this mornin. He's lookin a bittie Breider.'

Bricks
Any long-serving employee is said to be so devoted to the company that he is 'in wi the bricks'.

Brikks
Trousers. 'Stop the car, Ina. That's the loon spewed aa ower ma Sunday brikks.'

Brokeners
Broken biscuits. All bakers sold off flawed goods in bags for a few pennies per quarter-pound. They were bought mostly by children, but few adults were above sending the children out to buy brokeners for family consumption. This is the North-east, after all. 'Ay-ay, Mr Stuart. Ony brokeners?' Note that grocers were often asked for **crackit eggs**, **chippit aeples** or **fadit chocolate**, all self-explanatory.

Broonie
Any obsequious person who sucks up to authority in the cause of self-advancement (and we all know several of those). 'That's an affa quick promotion young Ian's got, isn't it?' 'He's a bit o a broonie, hid ye nae noticed?' Derives presumably from 'brown-noser', meaning that the individual is not shy of sticking his nose up the boss's behind if it results in a title. Such people are also **sooks**.

Brose
Oatmeal and salt, mixed vigorously with boiling water. Once the staple diet of all North-east farmworkers, this thick, cloying gruel differs from porridge in that the only heat in the process is derived from the boiling water, so there is very little cooking, as such. Must be stirred thoroughly and quickly to avoid lumps, although many elderly North-easters insisted that the lumps were best. The stirring was done traditionally with a spoon handle. The bowl of the same spoon was later used to eat the mixture. Sunday brose was usually topped off with cream. Most men insisted that the best brose was the brose they made for themselves and that any third-party concoction was a pale imitation of the real thing. Hence '**a man steers his ain brose best**'.

Brosey
Of burly physical appearance. An English-speaker might say

'strapping'. 'Araminta's got hersel a brosey chiel for her latest fiancy.' A young woman of burly physical appearance is said to be 'a brosey deem'.

Bubbles
Nasal discharge of the peculiarly liquid variety exclusive to children. 'Come ower here, Jason, and grandma'll dicht yer bubbles.'

Buchanie
The *Buchan Observer*. Weekly paper which is required reading in and around its base of Peterhead. When a son or daughter of Buchan refers to the paper, he or she will usually refer to 'the Buchanie', but if in posh company might refer to it as the *Observer*. It takes guests a minute or two to understand that their hosts don't mean the prestigious Sunday paper published in London, but a more important community organ altogether.

Bucket
An excess of drink. Someone bordering on alcoholism is said to 'tak an affa bucket'.

Buckie
Any normally shy person who suddenly does something which draws attention to himself is said to be 'comin oot o his buckie'. A buckie is a whelk, and anyone familiar with the habits of a live whelk will understand the metaphor.

Buckshee
Describing anything which might be superfluous to requirements. 'Ony buckshee scraps for ma dog, butcher?'

Bugga
A bag of. 'Jean, that new frock maks ye look lik a bugga cats awa tae be droont.' A child who cannot be persuaded to sit still is said to behave 'lik a bugga rats'.

17

Buggerin
Not a sexual offence, but a particularly severe chastisement. 'I got an affa buggerin fae ma boss this mornin.'

Bumff
Not just unwanted mailshots, but also the elegant county town of the sadly dispatched county of Banffshire. Billy Connolly, who was once booed off the stage by the citizens thereof for misjudging their tastes and using his customary ripe material, railed in a subsequent interview that the town was well named. 'Bumff?' he said. 'It sounds like a fart in a wet paper bag.' Really, there was no need for that.

Bunnet
Headgear of the elderly male. 'I see Jim's got a new reid bunnet. It matches his een.' A particularly big and floppy example may be said to be a **doolander**, meaning that it would be wide enough for a doo (pigeon) to land on. Also . . .

Bunnet
Any elderly man wearing a flat cap. 'Fit wye are we stuck in a queue o sivventeen cars traivellin at twinty-fower mile an oor?' 'There'll be a bunnet drivin the car at the front.'

Burst
Unsuccessful. 'Only twa numbers on the Lottery this wikk. The game's a burst.' Also, *to buy something with a large-denomination banknote.* 'I doot I'll hae tae burst this twinty-poun note.' And *to cut the first slice from some well-presented pie.* 'It's a shame tae burst a new pavlova.'

Burstin
Desperate to urinate or defecate. 'Are ye nearly finished in there? I'm burstin oot here.'

Buttery
The key to a quintessential North-east breakfast. Flour, lard and salt

18

are mixed and cut into random shapes roughly three inches in diameter. They are baked and the results can be spread with butter or margarine, jam or syrup. You can almost hear the calories, but there's little more satisfying or comforting to a homesick North-east person. Few holidaymakers going off to stay with North-east exiles are not begged to bring a couple of dozen butteries. The rubbish baked in the South for chainstores and supermarkets, most of which are sealed in fours in plastic wrapping before being imported to the North-east, are shabby impostors and should be avoided. Buttery is the rural word. Aberdonians know a buttery as a **rowie** (qv).

Byoch
Bring up wind. This verb can also be a noun. Both are clearly onomatopoeic, as you'll understand if you try saying it. 'Granda tried a suppie pasta for his tea and he's been byochin in front o the TV aa nicht.' See also **Rift**.

By-the-by
By the way. Favoured conversational ploy in which one party thinks of a last-minute subject which needs airing immediately. 'Weel, cheerio Rona. Oh, by the by, hiv ye heard aboot Elsie's man?'

By-the-way
A Glaswegian. Not much puzzle here; this affectionate term from the sons and daughters of the Dear Green Place was coined because of their alleged fondness for 'by the way' as a suffix to many conversational sentences, viz: 'That wis nivver a penalty, ref, by the way.' If the Glasgow Fair fortnight still delivered hordes of tourists to Aberdeen Beach instead of to Florida and Majorca, Aberdonians would declare that 'ye canna get moved on the Prom for by-the-ways'. In the interests of balance and national harmony, I should admit that Glaswegians are said to refer to Aberdonians as Furryboots, allegedly because of our citizens' curiosity about strangers, as in: 'Furryboots are you fae?' Complete nonsense.

C

Ca a man til his grave
Enough to kill someone. Could be used of any wearying situation, I suppose, but used most commonly in wartime Aberdeen of a woman who liked to play the field while her husband was away in the Services. Older Aberdonians still use it of flighty females. 'That lassie's jist like her grunnie. Baith o them wid ca ony man til his grave.'

Cackit up
Charged. 'The grocer cackit me up twa poun for a half-dizzen peaches.'

Cadder
Money. This was borderline for inclusion in the book, because the word is almost dead. Most elderly North-east people refer to money as 'siller'. Cadder seems to be a Kincardine word, used most in the Laurencekirk area. 'I canna be deein wi door-tae-door collections. Fowk's nivver deen sikkin cadder.'

Cairry
An off-licence carryout or *a helping hand with a burden.* 'Get's a cairry o a dizzen exports.' 'Wid ye gie's a cairry doon the stairs wi this aul bedstead?'

Cake
A block of soap. No one buys or uses a bar of soap in the North-east. We use 'cakes'. 'Is there anither cake o Wright's Coal Tar aneth the sink?'

Calved
See **Drappit**.

Cappie
Ice-cream cone. 'Awa doon til the shoppie and get's a coupla cappies.' A cappie with a Cadbury's Flake rammed into its centre is a Ninety-nine.

Car queen
Female teenager who picks her boyfriends according to the status of the young man's car. Car queens may be seen on most Friday and Saturday nights in the passenger seats of Escorts, Astras and Fiestas making largely pointless journeys up and down the streets of North-east towns and villages. Since the purpose is to be noticed, the car's interior lights are usually switched on and the windows are wound down no matter how inclement the weather so that all passers-by and residents may benefit from the WUMP-WUMP-WUMP of the in-car stereo system. See also **Car-park bandit**.

21

Carl-doddie

A particular form of rib grass (Plantago lanceolata) which North-east children use to play a game similar to conkers. Each player holds a stalk and takes alternate turns to try to knock the head off the other person's grass. The name is more than 250 years old, dating from the time of Bonnie Prince Charlie (Carl) and King George II (Doddie).

Car-park bandit

Any young blade who spends as many leisure hours as possible sitting in his car in a village car-park. Car-park bandits may be seen in corners of most community car-parks, parked driver's door to driver's door with the windows wound down. These conversations are punctuated occasionally by roaring off to whizz two or three times round the car-park or once up and down the village main street before returning to the same car-park corner to continue the conversation. See also **Car queen**.

Cartoon

Container for holding liquids or loose items. Nothing to do with Porky Pig or Tom and Jerry. This is the North-east's version of carton, I suppose. 'I see they're even sellin soup in cartoons noo.'

Cas-ash

Casino Cinema, one-time entertainment magnet in Wales Street, near Aberdeen Beach, now but a distant memory. 'Fit's on at the Cas-ash? North by North-west starrin Cary Grant? He's an affa Cary, is he?'

Cat's sookins

A particularly lank hairdo. 'Ethel peyed aa that money for a perm and it's come oot lik cat's sookins.' An agricultural equivalent is: 'Hair lik straa blaain aff a midden.' See also **Hingin mince**.

Cattie's faces

Item of North-east bakery popular until the 1960s. A sweet bun roughly 12 inches. in diameter was marked into eighths before

Cat's Sookins

baking. When pulled from the oven, it was sprinkled with sugar and each eighth could be torn off cleanly and sold individually. The resulting triangular shape of each piece was not unlike a cat's face. 'I'll tak twa bradies, a tattie scone, fower French cakes and twa cattie's faces.'

CBE
A lazy person. 'There's Ernie Buchan, CBE.' The CBE stands for Canna Be Ersed (*Can't be bothered*).

Ceemetry
Graveyard. 'Ma mither wis makkin jam at the wikkend. She sent me up til the ceemetry for jars.'

Chaa yer lugs
Chew your ears. Usually the first sign of a spat developing, when one party becomes increasingly exasperated with the other party's conversation, manner or boasting and erupts with: 'Awa and chaa yer lugs!'

A change o loaf
Often used to sum up a less-than-successful day out, whereby the highlight was the purchase of a loaf at the destination town's bakery. 'Weel, I've hid better days oot, bit at least it wis a change o loaf.'

Chappin
Knocking. Used in the game of dominoes by any player who cannot make a move with the tiles left in his hand, but also increasingly used of anyone who has reached an impasse. 'We've burst twa tyres, run oot o petrol and we're twelve mile fae the nearest village. We're chappin and nae mistake.'

Check
Encouragement to observe something surreptitiously, usually because it's a likely source of humour. 'Check the boy's haircut.' 'Check the dame's frock.'

China cabinet
The centrepiece of any respectable pensioner's front room. This display
cabinet contains all manner of ornaments, family photographs,
collectors' teaspoons from foreign climes and the best china.
Cabinet and contents are dusted lovingly and reverentially each day.

Chipper
Chip shop. Always 'the chipper', never 'the chippie'. 'That new
manager at the chipper changes his fat ilky sax month whether it
needs it or no.' North-east chippers are responsible for such delights
as pineapple fritters, haggis suppers, mock chops and the quintessential 1990s delicacy, the deep-fried Mars Bar.

Choobs
The human insides, otherwise known as guts. Derives from 'tubes'.
'I've been up aa nicht, doctor. Terrible bothered wi ma choobs.' Less
polite society refers to this as **poodins**.

Christmas
A gift given on December 25. Few North-east people receive
Christmas presents. We receive 'wir Christmas', as in: 'Fit did ye get
for yer Christmas, Gibby?' A similar all-purpose inquiry would be:
'Wis Sunty good tae ye?'

Chuckies
Small granite stones used to surface driveways throughout Scotland.
Almost all come from quarries around the North-east. They may be
grey or pink and come in several sizes. 'It'll tak twa larryloads o
chuckies tae cover yer yard, missus.'

Chucks
Choux pastry. Derived, presumably, from pronouncing the word as
it looks. 'I prefer Chalmers' chocolate eclairs. Their chucks disna
taste o lard.'

Chuddie
Chewing-gum. 'There's nithing as orra as lassies chaain chuddie in the street.'

Chum
To seek a favour. 'If ye chum Bob, he'll maybe gie ye a shot o his Rotavator.'

Cinema One
West Chapel at Aberdeen Crematorium. A term coined, as far as I am aware, by the *Scotland the What?* crew members. If they didn't invent it, they certainly popularised it.

Cinema Two
East Chapel, as above.

Claa far it's nae yokie
Scratch where it isn't itchy. Said of anyone who has been taken down a peg or two, or who has been given cause to think twice about himself and his behaviour. 'That'll gaur him claa far it's nae yokie.'

Clae-davies
Coarse-cloth trousers favoured by older generations of farmworkers because of their durability. 'See Erchie's clae-davies? He's worn them since he got them at Heppie's in the year o the Coronation.'

Claik
Gossip, or one who gossips. 'Fit's yer claik, Ina?' 'Dinna set me next tae Mrs Farquhar; she's an affa claik.' Along most of Donside, the word 'claik' becomes 'sclaik', defined in exactly the same way.

Clap
To pet or stroke an animal. 'Awa and gie the doggie a clap, dearie. On ye go, it winna hurt ye. Ay, ye're safe enough. He's affa

26

gweednatered. Go on, gie't a clappie. That's the stuff.' CRUNCH
'Quick! Somebody phone for a doctor!'

Clappit in
Anyone who has removed his false teeth is said to have a clappit-in
face.

Clappit thegither
Thrown together. Used mostly of sandwiches: 'Twa bits o loaf spread
wi jam and clappit thegither.' But also used for anything which has
been prepared carelessly. 'James, your ink exercise is one of the worst
this school has seen. Simply clappit thegither, if I may say so.' And:
'I doot she got dressed in the dark this mornin. Her claes wis jist
clappit thegither.'

Clart
As a noun, this is farmyard mud. As a verb, it means to plaster on
thickly. Thus, the noun: 'Ye'll need yer weldies (qv) oot in the fairm
close the day; there's an affa clart.' And the verb: 'Thon deemie
clarts on her make-up lik plaster.' Note that a particularly stupid
person is said to be 'as thick as clart in a bottle', which is very
colourful, but I'm not sure what it means. Anyone with muddy
shoes would be admonished with: **'Yer beets is clartit in dubs.'** '*Your
boots are plastered with mud.*' Since clart and dubs mean the same
thing, this is an example of North-east tautology, or North-east
emphasis, depending on your point of view.

Clatt
Much undersung hamlet between Alford and Huntly, famed for an
old farming joke in which a woman cyclist supposedly arrives at an
unsignposted fork in the road and stops a passing farmer to ask:
'Excuse me, is this the wye tae Clatt?' 'Michty,' says the farmer, 'if
ye claa't that wye ye'll caa't deen.' I'm not explaining.

Cleg
Horse-fly. An insect to be avoided at all costs for its painful bite

27

which leaves a permanent mark. Many North-east inhabitants can point to raised pale spots and tell a tale of a cleg bite 40 years before.

Clockie
A prominent fixture at the Beach Ballroom, Aberdeen. Beaux and belles usually agreed to meet each other 'aneth the clockie' prior to an evening's dancing. This was not always an astute arrangement. So many couples agreed to meet aneth the clockie that often hundreds of lost souls were milling about there looking in vain for their clicks, while the dancefloor inside remained comparatively barren. Note that in some parts of rural Aberdeenshire, a clock is still referred to as a **k-nock**. 'Fit's the time, Jean? I canna see the k-nockie fae here.'

Clockin
Clucking. A broody hen is said to be 'a clockin hennie', but the word can also be used of a fussing old gossip who can't stop talking. 'Sorry I'm late; I fell in wi the wifie Robertson doon the road and ye ken fit she's like for clockin.' This probably led to the Scots variation, claikin (qv). Also, any spinster who feels that life and men are passing her by and is desperate for an engagement ring is said to be 'clockin'.

Clubbie book
Home-shopping catalogue. This method of shopping found its niche in the cost-conscious North-east because it allowed clients to pay for an item (usually ill-fitting clothes) for mere pennies each week. Daring clients approaching a night out with nothing decent to wear usually buy a party frock from the clubbie book, wear it to the function, then employ the firm's returns policy to get their money back.

Clubbie-book bride
Oriental wife of a Scottish husband. 'Oot tae Bangkok on a fortnicht's holiday and there's him back wi a clubbie-book bride.'

28

Clypie-clypie clashbags
Playground cry of outrage, always directed at the class telltale or teacher's pet, usually one and the same person.

Coalie-back
Piggyback. This Aberdonian word is derived from the days of street coalmen carrying sacks of coal on their backs. 'Ye've been oot on that back green giein the kids coalie-backs for the last twa oors. Ye're a bigger bairn than they are.' See also **Horsie-back**.

Cocky Hunter's
Celebrated Aberdeen emporium. It lay just beyond the eastern end of Union Street and its stock was displayed in no particular order so that, even on good days, it looked as if a bomb had hit. The store has long since closed and the site has been redeveloped but, even now, any home or office which badly needs tidying up is said to 'look lik Cocky Hunter's'. The name lives on in a pub at the other end of Union Street.

Codona's
A funfair. The family name of the company which operates the funfair at Aberdeen Beach and which can claim several crowd-pulling attractions. Now used increasingly by many Aberdonians as a generic term for any fairground, funfair or theme park. At this rate, it won't be long before North-east tourists return from Florida or California reporting that they spent most of their time in 'thon Codona's wi the Mickey Moose'.

Collie's
Top-class grocery in Union Street, Aberdeen, now closed. Say 'Collie's' to any North-east person over 50 and they'll reply: 'Oh, the smell of the coffee.' This grocery and delicatessen was celebrated not just in Aberdeen but throughout Scotland for the breadth of its produce and the quality of its stock. The trademark smell of fresh-ground coffee pervaded a large stretch of the top end of Union Street. Collie's was the sort of shop which any major city sacrifices

when it succumbs to anodyne shopping malls and chainstores. These national names suck a community's money elsewhere and turn a city's distinctive character into the same bland facelessness of every other place in the UK. I'm allowed one rant a book, and that was it.

Come ower ye
Befall you. 'Drive slow and nithing'll come ower ye.' Any child who is crying bitterly for no apparent reason will be told: 'Michty, michty. Fit's adee? There's nithing comin ower ye.'

Committee
Nothing unusual here, but the North-east pronunciation puts the stress on the last syllable. 'The committ*ee* wid like tae thank Mr Robbie Shepherd for his comments.' Note that 'comm*ents*' also takes the stress on the last syllable.

Confirmed interrogative
Another curious feature of Aberdeen grammar in which the speaker asks a question and promptly answers it himself. 'Did ye enjoy yer holidays, ay?' 'Did ye nae find fit ye wis lookin for, no?' 'Are ye burstin for the lavvie, ay?' 'Did she nae offer ye a lift hame, no?'

~~Co-opie Doug~~
Still revered by many as probably the best, most hospitable and most honest shopowner and salesman the North-east has produced. The late Douglas Anderson operated the Mossat Shop, between Alford and Strathdon, until the early 1970s. His prices were not particularly keen, but people flocked in from a 50- or 60-mile radius, especially on Sundays, for the experience of buying something from Co-opie Doug. Frequently, a family would sit down after Sunday lunch and wonder what they would do to fill the afternoon. Eventually, someone would suggest: 'Come on and we'll awa tae Co-opie Doug's.' His nickname came from the fact that he served his time as a grocer at the Scottish Co-operative Wholesale Society at Alford, although it could equally have come from the fact

that his own shop's stock was so broad that it rivalled a Co-opie. A similarly famed North-east emporium was McIntosh of Forgue, which carried so many lines that a modern hypermarket would be shamed.

Co-opie loaf
Pregnant. Bread from the old Co-operative Society bakery in Aberdeen was said to be unusually doughy and liable to swell in the stomach. Hence, a woman in the early stages of pregnancy might be hailed with: 'Fan are ye due? Or is it Co-opie loaf?' That's the Aberdeen expression. The rural one is: '**Hiv ye been aetin new tatties?**'

Coorse
Bad, coarse or awkward. Another multipurpose Doric word, illustrated best by examples. 'He's been coorse the hale holidays. I'll be gled fin the school starts again.' 'This is gey coorse material for curtains. Hid they nithing bonnier?' 'Gie's the little spanner ower here, this nut's real coorse tae shift.'

Coorse as cat's dirt
Utterly foul. What was once the most pervasive and malodorous contamination known to North-east farm wives, cat poop, lives on in this expression for anything and anyone that is decidedly less than appealing. 'Heaven knows fit wye he took up wi her; she's as coorse as cat's dirt.'

Coo's fit
Cow's foot. Another name for the pastry-and-icing confection otherwise known as bloomers (qv). As well as the shape resembling a voluminous pair of drawers hanging on the washing-line, its outline looks equally like the imprint of a cloven hoof in mud. 'I'll tak half a dizzen coo's feet and three o yer baps, baker.'

Coo's lick
An unruly tuft of hair running against the grain at the forward

hairline, found usually in primary schoolboys. 'Oor Cedric's school photie wis spiled because his teacher nivver thocht tae gie his coo's lick a weet dicht.'

Coup-the-ladle
Playground see-saw. 'Ronnie fell aff the coup-the-ladle and clattered his heid aff the cement. Efter extensive tests at the hospital, it's been scientifically proven that his IQ's up twenty-nine points.' The 'coup' is pronounced 'cowp'. Despite best researches, none of my contacts has any idea of the derivation. It might have something to do with ladling soup from a broth pot and spilling the contents, but I'll take advice.

Cove
One of many Banffshire words for an individual, or chiel. 'Far are ye gaun the day, cove?' See also **Gade, Gadgie** and **Min**.

Crackit chuntie
Damaged chamberpot. Anyone whose singing voice is not what it might be is said to have 'a voice lik a crackit chuntie'. The same voice might also be described as '**lik a roosty razor**'.

Craigie
Aberdeen Prison, Craiginches. Many an unruly Aberdonian child was threatened with a spell in Craigie, that forbidding granite fortress on the edge of Torry, high above the lower reaches of the River Dee. Alas, the threat must have been used too infrequently, for a high proportion of Her Majesty's guests are former young Aberdeen blades.

Craiter
Creature. Unlike the rest of Scotland, this has nothing to do with whisky, which the rest of Scotland spells *cratur,* anyway. Whisky in the North-east is a sweelie, a sensation, a something, or just a plain old dram. No, a craiter is a poor, frail unfortunate, usually of

pension age. 'Look at that peer aul craiter ower the road.' This led to the tame schoolboy joke: 'Why should you feel sorry for the moon?' 'Because it's filled wi aul craters.' It wasn't funny in 1965, either.

Crem
Crematorium. 'There's something affa caul aboot a funeral at the Crem.'

Creamola Foam
Scottish-made fizzy-drink crystals. Sold in very small tins with prise-off lids. To the best of my recollection, the three flavours available were strawberry, lemon and orange. Any mother who hoped for peace and quiet during 1960s school holidays knew to lay in supplies.

Crikey dicks!
All-purpose exclamation. 'Crikey dicks! It's yersel. I thocht ye wis deid.'

Crochlie
Frail. The CH is pronounced as in LOCH. 'She got oot o the hospital on Tuesday. They pit them hame far ower early nooadays, so she's still a bittie crochlie.' Literally, crochlie is a disease causing lameness in cattle.

Crunk her up!
An encouragement to renewed and greater effort. Derived from the days when pushbikes were ubiquitous in rural Scotland and anyone dallying would be exhorted to pedal faster or 'crunk her up'. In farming areas of the North-east, the saying was embellished to: 'Crunk her up! Ye'll seen hae butter.' – an allusion to hand-cranked butter churns. Also, anyone using one of the old starting-handles to fire up a stubborn car might have been urged to 'crunk her up'. Nowadays, 'crunk her up' is not limited to cycling or cars. Any

33

North-east boss will encourage his indigenous staff by advising them to 'crunk her up'. As in: 'Crunk her up or we'll nivver get this order oot.'

A cuppa tea and a cairry-on
Standard Aberdeen reply to the question: 'Fit will we dee the nicht?'

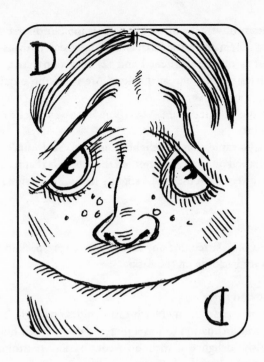

D

Daily
*A noun which might refer to any daily newspaper, but most commonly
means the Press and Journal, Britain's biggest and oldest regional
morning newspaper.* 'Did ye see that story in the daily the day?'

Darker
A blind rage. From the younger end of the social spectrum in the
North-east. 'Kylie's boyfriend got aff wi Zoë on Friday nicht. What
a darker Kylie took. Zoë needed stitches.'

Darkie John
Any door-to-door salesman originally from the Indian sub-continent.

These salesmen were common throughout the North-east until the late 1960s. The name is used hardly at all nowadays, because (1) the North-east is more enlightened and (2) they don't exist, anyway. 'Mam! That's Darkie John at the door! Are ye needin onything the day?'

Dash the bit
An idiomatic expression of delighted surprise. Said usually in conversation, when one party has amused the other. 'Is that really fit she said? Weel, weel, dash the bit.' A slightly less polite version is '**damn the linth**'.

Daskie
Pew in church. 'Darren; for ony sake show some respeck in the kirk and keep yer backside on the daskie.'

Days here and there
Stay-at-home holiday. Many North-east families on a tight budget or with no great inclination to travel prefer to devote their holidays to exploring the delights of their own countryside, returning home each night and setting off again in a different direction the next morning. 'Far are ye gaun for yer hol'days, Winnie?' 'Och, days here and there.'

The Deaths
Daily column of obituary notices in the Press and Journal. Required reading for every North-east person over 40. Its move from Page Two of the paper to a position near the paper's centre caused the biggest howl of outrage any *Press and Journal* editor has weathered in 75 years. 'Did ye see fa wis in The Deaths the day, Chrissie?'

Deid
Beyond redemption. 'That's you deid fin the boss finds oot.'

Dell
To dig. 'Faither's oot dellin the back gairden.' Also, anyone spotted

36

swinging the lead or otherwise idling while any form of work lies undone is admonished with: 'Hey min, that's nae dellin.' (That's not getting anything dug over).

Diary
Where cows are milked or milk products are sold. Among older North-east people, a diary is very rarely a daily journal of personal thoughts. 'I'm makkin a trifle for wir denner, Sandy. Awa doon til the diary and get a pint o double cream.'

Dicht yer feet
Ubiquitous instruction to any visitor to make sure that his shoes are clean before he ventures inside.

Diminutive
A curious grammatical feature of the North-east dialect, in which most concrete and abstract nouns are given their diminutive form. One does not go for a Sunday run, one goes for a Sunday runnie. One does not open a tin of beans, one opens a tinnie. One does not clean the front steps, one cleans the steppies. These diminutives are applied irrespective of the scale or size of the noun which they modify. Thus, a Sunday jaunt from Aberdeen to Inverness, then to Wick, to Durness, down to Fort William, on to Perth and back to Aberdeen, would amount to more than 700 miles and would still be just 'a fine runnie'.

Dinna droon the miller
'Not too much water in my whisky, if you please.' The miller is a refer-ence to the grain in a dram.

Dinna gee yer ginger
Keep calm. Comes from the fact that fresh-ground ginger is such a powerful spice that anyone who overindulges moves a good deal faster. Similarly: **Keep a calm sooch** (CH pronounced as in Loch).

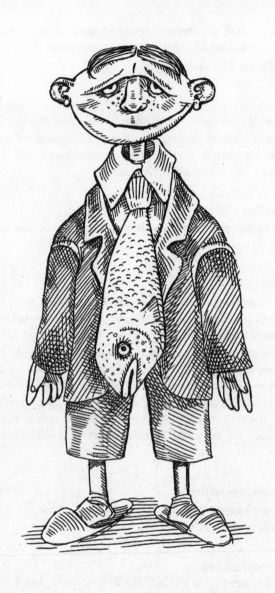

Dippie

Dippie
Anyone with a lazy eyelid. Rather a cruel term deriving from the full expression 'dippit heidlichts' (dipped headlights).

Dirdin on
Struggling by. 'Foo are ye deein, Wattie?' 'Och, dirdin on, dirdin on.' Similar to **tyauvin**.

Dirler
Toilet. Derived from the days of enamel chamberpots, which, when used as intended, clattered and drummed, or 'dirled'. 'Ma sister canna come tae the phone; she's on the dirler.'

Dirt-deen
Exhausted. 'I'm awa til ma bed; I'm jist dirt-deen.'

Divv
Any young woman whose hold on reality is tenuous. 'She's covered her bedroom wa wi posters o Des O'Connor. What a divv.' Might derive from the word **Divot**, which is also used as an insult. An alternative word is **spoon**.

Dock
Not the ubiquitous broad-leaved weed (which is a docken) but the human hindquarters. Used most often when threatening a small child with corporal punishment, as in: 'Jason, if ye dinna get doon aff that wa this minute, ye'll get a skelpit dock.' Note: in some parts of Aberdeenshire, a skelpit dock is also known as a **Sconed Dock**, perhaps because a baker working up a good scone or bannock dough gives the dough a good battering. I'll take advice.

Docken
Broad-leaved weed. Anything which is utterly worthless is said to be 'nae worth a docken'.

Doh

An unco-operative person. This is probably the newest example of North-east vernacular in this book, because it comes from an eight-year-old. 'If I canna hae a sweetie, ye're jist a doh.'

Doms

Age-old pub game in which black tiles with white spots are abutted in sequence. Known everywhere else as dominoes. 'Get's baith a drammie, Jock, and I'll tak ye on at the doms.' Occasions great elation wherever played, so on no account to be confused with . . .

Dons

Aberdeen Football Club. 'I see the Dons hiv signed anither dud.' The name might be a contraction of 'Aberdonians' or might have something to do with the River Don, one of the two rivers on which the city stands.

Doocot

Pigeon loft, but also *any small cupboard or gloryhole (qv) in a house or office.* 'We keep the stationery in the grey doocot.'

Dookers

Swimming costume. 'We'll hae a runnie tae Banff Links the morn. Mind and tak yer dookers.'

Doon aboot the moo

Down about the mouth. Out of sorts. 'Mercy, Violet, ye've surely hid bad news. Ye're lookin real doon aboot the moo.'

Doon Mac's hole in America

Final response by an exasperated adult to a child's repeated questions about the location of some item, person or place. 'Far's ma sweeties, dad?' 'Nivver mind.' 'Far's ma sweeties, dad?' 'I couldna say.' 'Bit far's ma sweeties, dad?' 'Och! Doon Mac's hole in America!'

Doon tae the herber
Down to the harbour. Said as a joke by anyone who finds that they can't afford something. 'Weel, it's doon tae the herber for me.' The implication is that prostitution is the only way to come up with ready funds.

Doon the Toon
Totally devoid of class. 'I've jist met ma loon's girlfriend for the first time. She's Doon the Toon, and nae mistake.' Or: 'I see Ina's got a Spanish flamenco-dancer doll in her front windae. Isn't that richt Doon the Toon?'

Doon throwe it
Anyone who attempts to speak BBC English having been brought up with pure Doric runs the risk of 'fa'in doon throwe it'. This is regarded as a mortal sin in the North-east, akin to betraying one's roots and not even succeeding at it. 'Did ye see Mima on the TV last nicht; tried tae lay on the pan-loff (qv), but kept fa'in doon throwe it?' Throwe is pronounced to rhyme with 'cow'. My favourite doon-throwe story concerns a countrywoman whose husband made good and bought a house in a posh part of Aberdeen. The minister came to call, but was being pestered by a gang of ragamuffins as he parked his car. The hostess was horrified and shouted: 'You ruffians! Away home to your mithers! Come away inside for your tea, minister. And don't bother your erse with them.'

Dose o the munchies
Ravenously hungry. An expression among North-east teens and twenties. 'I've been oot playin fitba a' aifterneen and I've got a terrible dose o the munchies.'

Dother
Daughter. 'Jack's dother's mairriet Bill's dother's loon and they'd twa dothers themsels.' Anyone who has listened to two or three North-

east women trying to sort out any family's lineage will know how confusing it can be without my trying to explain the process.

Dottled
Elderly and confused. 'Wid ye look in on Mrs Jamieson fae time tae time? She's gettin a bittie dottled.'

Doughballs
Flour-margarine-and-water lumps found as an accompaniment to a pan of mince. Like **skirlie**, born of days when meat was so expensive that it had to be stretched (made to go further). The uncooked lumps of dough are cooked as the mince simmers, and they swell in the heat. Of no nutritional value whatsoever, but their texture is curiously cloying and comforting. A doughball is also another name for a stupid person.

Dowp
Bum. 'Her dowp's that big. If she sits on a stool, maist o't sits on the fleer.' 'Ye wid think somebody wi a dowp lik that widna weer track-suit bottoms.' Anyone with an especially prominent beam end is said to sport a **pelmet**. A pelmet can also be an exceptionally short skirt.

Dowpie
Cigarette end. See **Tabbie**.

Dowpit
Shapeless in the seat. Any trousers or slacks which are so worn or are of such poor manufacture that they lose all shape in the behind are said to be dowpit. The word can also be used of anyone who walks with his backside protruding. Hence: 'If Frunk disna stop walkin sae dowpit, aa his brikks'll be dowpit.'

Drappit
Given birth. Not a particularly attractive or respectful term for the miracle of human life, but one rooted in the farm tradition of the North-east. Not often heard nowadays, apart from among diehard

Doricists well past pension age. 'Weel, loon, I wis hearin ye'll be a faither shortly. Or his she drappit already?' Travelling people in the North-east have a lovely philosophical turn of phrase for the trauma of an overdue birth. Quite unperturbed, they observe: **'Fin an aipple's ripe, it fa's.'**

Dreel

A row of vegetables in agriculture or horticulture. 'Foo many dreel o tatties this 'ear, Sandy?' Note: to **'trump the dreel'** is to be stuck in a rut. 'I've been trumpin this dreel for five 'ear noo. I doot it's time for a change.' The plural of dreel is still dreel.

Dubs at ilky door

Mud at every door. Doric's way of saying that everyone has their problems, secrets or faults. Another such phrase is: **'There's aye a muckle slippery steen at ilky body's door.'**

Dumplins bilin ower

Used of any woman of ample bosom or who is wearing a dangerously low-cut dress.

Dungars

Overalls. Short for dungarees. 'Ye're nae deein the gairden in yer gweed brikks. Come inside and pit on yer dungars.'

Dunt

A blow, but also *redundancy* or *sacking.* 'Some gawpit so-and-so's duntit the side o ma car in the car-park.' 'That's me hame early, petal. I've got the dunt.'

Dwaublie

Unsteady. 'She faintit twinty minutes back and she's still a bittie dwaublie.'

Dwaumie

A fainting spell. Can also be used of someone who has not been paying attention. 'Ma mither took a dwaumie at the sink last nicht and we'd tae get the doctor'. Or: 'Davidson! Pay attention up at the back there! You're away in a dwaumie!'

Dweeb
Any studious young person. Other generations would know such people as swots. Americans call them nerds. The younger Northeast generation knows them as dweebs. 'Perry's that much o a dweeb that he sleeps wi his chemistry books.'

Dykesider
Any child or adult known to have been conceived out of wedlock, supposedly because their parents consummated a lightning attraction wherever any modicum of privacy could be found, usually, given the nature of North-east social life and the fierceness of the illicit hormonal rush, behind a dyke.

E

Eachy, peachy

Playground rhyme for choosing participants in a game. The full title is 'Eachy, peachy, peary, plum'. You don't need me to give you the second line, but it involves a potato and proves that the North-east's peculiar obsession with bodily cavities begins at an early age.

Echt

Aberdeenshire hamlet between Tarland and Aberdeen, and also the Doric word for the number eight. The *Press and Journal* sports department lives for the day when the football teams of Echt and Fyvie meet in a high-scoring match and the result can be reported: Echt five, Fyvie echt.

Echt

Education, Salvation and Damnation
The Aberdeen nickname given to the triumvirate of granite buildings standing side by side at the far end of Union Terrace Gardens: the Central Library, St Mark's Church and His Majesty's Theatre.

Eeksie-peeksie
Equal. 'That's a lucky tattie for you, Jason. And a lucky tattie for you, Kylie. That's the twa o ye eeksie-peeksie.'

Ee'll be different
You'll be different. A catch-all defence often used by exasperated parents, viz: 'Mam, can I hae an ice-cream?'
    'No.'
    'Mam, I'm really needin an ice-cream.'
    'I said No.'
    'Ackie Duncan's got an ice-cream, mam.'
    'Good for Ackie. Ee'll be different.'

Eese
Use. The abstract noun, not the verb. There are varying degrees of 'eese'. An item may be nae eese, nae muckle eese or, in extreme circumstances, nae bliddy eese ava.

Eetle-ottle
Another playground rhyme for choosing participants in a game. There are several versions, but the most common appears to have been: 'Eetle-ottle. Black bottle. Eetle-ottle. OUT.'

Erse
Not Irish Gaelic; this is the backside of anything animate or inanimate, but usually human. The more I researched this book, the more I realised that the Doric would be completely lost if this word did not exist. To give just one example, anyone who has made a bad fist of any task is said to have 'made an erse o't' (made a backside of it). There are dozens more.

Ersefae o mud-geards
A colourful warning to someone straying too far off the pavement, common in the days when bicycles were more frequent than cars and there were many collisions between cyclists and pedestrians, hence: 'Come awa fae that road, Kylie. Ye'll get an ersefae o mud-geards.'

F

Face

The North-east has never been overly concerned with facial aesthetics, hence our myriad ways of describing them, as in:

A face like the back o the lum.

A face like a bag o bruised fruit.

A face like a bashed chuntie.

A face like a biled thripny.

A face like a burst melodeon.

A face like a burst settee.

A face like a flittin.

A face like a hairst meen (harvest moon).

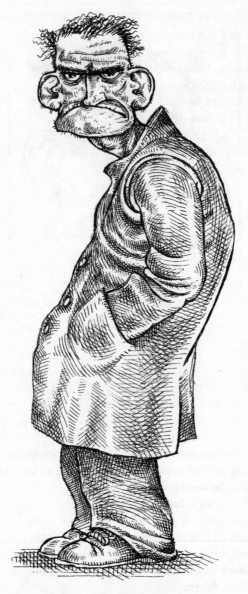

Face Like a Burst Settee

A face like a hen layin razors.

A face like a saft tattie.

A face like a skelpit erse.

A face like a skittery hippen (soiled nappy).

A face like a torn scone.

A face like a turkey cock.

A face like a weel-kickit ba.

A face like a weet nicht lookin for a dry mornin.

A face like a weet washin.

Face aa roon

Face all round. Disingenuous. Wilfully misleading. 'I'm nae carin if Florrie telt ye yer new frock suitit ye. Ye should ken Florrie's face aa roon.' The implication is that Florrie presents a different face to different people.

Falsers

Dentures. 'I see the wifie twa doors doon's got new falsers. She's got a smile lik the Union Street fairy lichts.'

Fancy piece

Not a woman of free morals, but *a cream cake or any item of sweet patisserie*. 'I'll hae fower o yer fancy pieces, baker.' Can cause some confusion with people from outside the North-east. I was once in the company of a New Zealander, who was marvelling at the hospitality he was receiving while staying as a guest on a North-east farm, particularly when his hostess told him she hoped that he hadn't eaten too much on a day trip to Aberdeen because she had two fancy pieces waiting for him inside.

Farm name

Phenomenon by which North-east farmers are known not by their first names or surnames, but by a shortened version of the name of their principal farm. Thus, the farmer at Barehead would be Baries, the farmer at Brownmill would be Broonies, the farmer at Bogensharn would be Bogies and the farmer at Backhillock would be Backies. Thus, a mart conversation might run: 'Bogies, awa ower and see if Backies and Baries is comin for a platie o Broonie's wife's stovies.'

Farrer up the stair
Older. An older person might say to a younger: 'Trust me; I'm farrer up the stair than you.'

Farty watter
Carbonated mineral water. Perrier, Ramlösa and San Pellegrino might be de rigueur in the fashionable restaurants of Paris, London and New York but, I'm sorry, they're all farty watter in the Northeast. 'Hey, Jim! Sees twa lobster thermidor, a ninety-two Sancerre and a bottle o farty watter.'

Fash
To trouble or worry. 'Dinna fash yersel, Wullie. It's nae as bad as it looks. It's amazin fit they can shoo back on nooadays.' One who is troubled is said to be **fashious**. A minor drama blown into a crisis is said to be 'a fash aboot nithin'.

Fat as a butter ba
Exceptionally plump. Named for the hard sweets known these days as Butter Nuts. These are spherical with a distinct blush of colour about them and could be said to resemble the face of an obese person. 'What a change I see in Mary. Last Christmas, she wis as thin as a skinned rubbit (qv), noo she's as fat as a butter ba.'

Feech-up
Makeshift job. The CH is pronounced as in Loch. 'I'd only half a pun o nails and three lengths o fower-by-two. It'll dee for a shed door, I suppose, bit it's a bit o a feech-up.'

Feel
Nincompoop. 'He sleeps in a tint on the back green in the middle o winter. He wis aye a bit o a feel.' An exceptional nincompoop is a

52

feel gype. The best example of its use in literature comes from Jamie Fleeman, who worked for the Laird of Udny in the middle of the 18th century and was not quite as daft as he was cabbage-looking. He is supposed to have met one of the Laird of Udny's titled friends in the grounds of Udny Castle and to have inquired: 'I'm the Laird o Udny's feel. Fa's feel are ee?'

Feelin nae pain
Drunk to the point of being anaesthetised. 'We took him hame and left him on his doorstep. He wis feelin nae pain.'

Ficher
To fumble or tinker. One may ficher with an engine, a clock mechanism or anything intricate, but there's another, more amorous definition, overheard at the back of Ballater Picture House in the late 1940s, when a frustrated young female voice inquired in the darkness: 'Wullie, fit wye div ye nivver ficher wi me noo?'

Filled a holie
Filled a hole. At the end of any meal which has been judged neither too excessive nor too slight, someone will lean back and offer as approbation: 'Weel, that jist filled a holie.' The implication is that a gnawing vacant spot in the stomach has been satisfied to perfection.

Fillims
Cinema. North-east Scots have an inability to pronounce the word for 'moving pictures' in one syllable. 'Are ye gaun oot the nicht, Donald? The pub, maybe? The dancin? The fillims?'

Fired legs
Rawness and tenderness of skin when wet clothes have been worn for too long. Applies mostly to hillwalkers and to small children pre-1970s who wet themselves at school because they were too scared to ask permission to leave the room. 'I'm gaun up tae sort oot that teacher

wifie the morn. That's the loon hame wi fired legs for the third day in a row.'

Fishwife
Any woman of abrasive nature, behaviour and vocabulary.

Fit?
What? All interrogative pronouns which begin in English with WH, begin with F in the Doric (Fit? Fa? Foo? Fan? Fit wye? Far?). This lends the Doric speaker a delicious crispness when confronted by pomposity. 'You have to understand, Mr Duncan, that due to the intrinsic peculiarities of the socio-economic climate in the current budgetary period, the strictures of Government block-grant policy vis-a-vis local authorities entails my declining your thoroughly apposite request to have an inside toilet fitted in the abode in which you currently reside.'
'Fit?'

Fit like?
How are you? The quintessential North-east greeting, by which sons and daughters of the North-east recognise each other worldwide. No matter where on the globe the encounter might take place, those two words encapsulate the warp and weft of everywhere from Peterhead to Braemar, Laurencekirk to Lossiemouth. The customary reply is: 'Nae bad. Foo's yersel?'

Fit o Market Street
Sacked. From the days when the Employment Exchange was located at the bottom of Market Street, Aberdeen. 'Weel, that's me awa tae the fit o Market Street again. Lord knows fit I did wrang.' Or: 'If you're nae careful, my lad, ye'll be at the fit o Market Street in five minutes flat.'

Fit's yer news?
Friendly inquiry on meeting a regular acquaintance.

Fittie
The old fishing village of Footdee, now consumed by the spread of Aberdeen. Anyone who pronounces the name of this community as Footdee can be marked immediately as an incomer.

Five-minute silence
Aberdeen nickname for a weekly paper. See also **squeak**.

Flechie
Bed. 'Hermione! Get up oot o yer flechie this minute.' The CH is pronounced as in Loch. Also . . .

Flechie
Infested with parasites. 'It's high time that dog got a bath. There's nithing on fower legs mair flechie.' One of the finest characters of North-east fiction was Donovan Smith's eponymous tramp, Flechie Dode.

Flechie Belmont
Belmont Cinema. One of Aberdeen's first picture palaces, long since disappeared from Belmont Street. It was never known for outstanding hygiene, hence its affectionate nickname.

Flee ceemetry
Fly cemetery – a pastry in which sweet mincemeat is sandwiched between two squares of pastry. One need only see one to understand how it got its name. Marginally tastier than it looks. Also known as a 'mucker'. You can imagine why.

Fleg
A scare. 'The gas oven gaed oot wi a bang this mornin. What a fleg I got.' Can also be a verb: 'Ma man loupit oot fae ahen the curtains and fleggit me.' 'Well, he's aye been a feel sumph, Iris.'

Fly cup
A social cup of tea, either at home or as a welcome rest on a day out.

The fly cup is the staple of North-east conviviality and can be as simple as a cup of tea on its own or, more usually, accompanied by handsome piles of biscuits, cakes or sandwiches. The 'fly' element has nothing to do with insects, but everything – at one time in the distant past, I suppose – to do with illicitness. 'Nellie? I hinna seen ye as lang time. Now ye'll jist come in for a fly cup and neen o yer nonsense.'

Foggieloan
Nickname for the Banffshire town of Aberchirder, shortened usually to just Foggie. Named for the peculiar mists which hang about the town, thanks to its topography, even when the surrounding countryside might be reasonably clear. The two names have caused some confusion, most notably when former police Chief Inspector Peter MacInnes was a young recruit awaiting a posting to a rural police station, and had heard bloodcurdling stories about what happened to young bobbies at Foggieloan. When he learned that he had been posted to Aberchirder, Peter told his young colleagues that he was relieved that he was not being posted to that terrible Foggieloan place.

Foo's aa wi ye?
How's everything with you? See **Fit like?**

Foo's yer doos?
Literally, *'How are your pigeons?'* A robust inquiry after one's health. Not used in polite company, because 'pigeons' is a synonym for bodily parts best kept hidden for fear of frightening the neighbours and small animals. The usual response to: 'Foo's yer doos?' is: 'Aye pickin.'

Fool
Not the English noun meaning 'idiot' (that's a gype), but an adjective meaning '*dirty*'. 'Dinna eat stuff that's been drappit on the fleer, dearie. It'll be fool.' A top-shelf magazine or much of Channel 4's late-night weekend programming could be said to be profoundly

fool or **orra** (qv). One of the old Aberdeen characters was a tramp known as Fool Friday. A Banffshire woman who is not particularly tidy or clean in her personal habits is a **fool maach** (CH pronounced as in loch). Her Aberdeenshire counterpart is a fool moch. A moch, by the way, is also a moth.

Fooshtie
Stale or *rancid*. 'That back room's needin a gweed airin. There's an affa fooshtie smell.' 'Pit oot that cheese; it's turned fooshtie.'

For
An inquiry as to what you might like. 'Fit are ye for tae yer tea the nicht?' 'Are ye for a skoof fae ma ale-bottle?'

Forkytail
Earwig. So named because of the twin pincers at the end of the insect's abdomen.

Free
Not gratis and for nothing (this is the North-east). Free means *runny* or *crumbly*. 'Yer jam hisna set affa weel, Teenie. It's real free, if ye dinna mind me sayin.' 'One bite o her Victoria sponge and it fell tae bits in ma lap. Onything as free as thon should nivver hiv won first prize. Still, I didna hae my cousin as the judge, did I?'

Froonyal
Funeral. A habitual North-east mispronunciation for the service of remembrance. 'That wis an affa nice froonyal yer mither got, Isa.' Conversely, a minister who is deemed to have put insufficient effort into dispatching the deceased with compassion and tribute to personal qualities will be said to have delivered: 'Nae froonyal ata. It could hiv been onybody lyin in thon box.'

Fry
A noun, not a verb, meaning *a small parcel of fish for cooking*. Few trips to the Banffshire or Aberdeenshire coast are complete without

stopping by a harbour and seeing if a fry is available direct from the boat or from the processor. Fish doesn't come any fresher. 'We gaed for a runnie tae Buckie and we've come back wi a fry for wir tea.' A boat crew will also take home a fry after a trip.

Fu as a puggie

Drunk. Comes from the childhood game of marbles, in which the puggie was the heeled indentation at which the marbles were aimed. When there were so many marbles in the target that no more could get in, it was 'fu'. Consequently, when someone has had so much to drink that he has room for not one more dram, he is 'as fu as a puggie'.

Full tae the pooch lids

Absolutely packed to bursting; literally, 'full to the tops of my pockets'. Full is pronounced to rhyme with hull, not bull. The phrase is said most often after Christmas lunch, when father leans back in his seat, claps either side of his expanding tum, and exclaims: 'Michty, I'm full tae the pooch lids.' One may also be said to be '**lip fu**'.

Funcies himsel

Fancies himself. Disparaging remark made of any young blade who has spent just a little too much time with the clothes, haircut, moisturiser, cologne and car. 'See wee Billy, dis he nae funcie himsel?' Also: 'If young Billy wis chocolate, he'd eat himsel.'

Fussle

To whistle or *a whistle* . 'Fussle yer doggie back here, Sandy.' 'C'mon ref, far's yer fussle!?' Perhaps used most poignantly in the tale of the young woman desperate for a date, who went to the hairdresser's specially to enhance her chances. The following morning, she was heard to remark: 'Twinty poun for a perm, and the only thing that fussled at me wis a seagull.'

Futret

Weasel. Emphatically not, as most of the North-east seems to think, a ferret. The word can also be used to describe a devious or duplicitous character. 'I canna stand next door's loon. There's something sleekit (qv) aboot him; jist a dampt futret.'

G

Gabby Aggie
Any talkative woman. 'Fit's Gabby Aggie sayin noo?'

Gad sakes
Squeamish expression of disgust. 'A caul-mince sandwich? Gad sakes.'
'My last boyfriend changed his draaers eence a wikk. Gad sakes.'

Gade
Banffshire word for any individual. 'Fit like the day, gade?' Similar
to . . .

Gadgie
Person. Also largely a Banffshire expression, although common in some parts of Buchan and Formartine. 'Look at the size o that gadgie's feet.'

Gaimrick
Any inhabitant of the Banffshire coastal village of Gardenstown, or the surrounding parish of Gamrie (pronounced Gaim-ray).

Gange
Prominent chin. 'The last time I saw a gange lik that wis on Desperate Dan.'

Gassed
Put at a disadvantage. 'They wheepit the wheels aff his car in the middle o the nicht, and him gaun on his holidays the next mornin. That wis him gassed.'

Gaun aa yer length
You're pushing your luck. 'Jist calm doon, Janet. Ye're gaun aa yer length.' The implication is that you're overstretching yourself to such a degree that you're exceeding your own height. Also, anyone who trips and falls prostrate is said to have 'gaen aa her length'.

Gaun yer dinger
To be very energetic. 'She did the hale spring-cleanin in twa days. She wis fairly gaun her dinger.'

Geets
Children, particularly misbehaving children. The G is hard. 'I'm aboot blue-heidit wi that barrafae o geets next door.' A particularly large assortment of children is said to be a '**squatter o geets**'.

Geil't
Frozen stiff. Pronounced as JEELT. 'Get oot o the front o that fire, Bertha. I stood waitin an oor for a bus and I'm geil't.' Note, one can

also be **geil't raa** (frozen raw) or **geil't tae the marra** (frozen to the core). Each is as unpleasant as the others.

Gettin aff at Blackfriars Street
The only form of contraception before the ready availability of condoms, known to the rest of the nation as the withdrawal method. Named after the Blackfriars Street bus stop, where most of the country buses from Donside and the North would discharge the last of their passengers before proceeding to the terminus at the Joint Station. Those who did not 'get aff at Blackfriars Street' had to go all the way to the bus garage and bear the consequences. Hence: 'Pregnant!? I canna be pregnant! Sandy got aff at Blackfriars Street!'

Gettin a turnie
Keeping busy. 'Hullo, Norman. Still gettin a turnie?'

Gey
Grammatical modifier meaning 'fairly'. Pronounced 'gye' (hard G). Used frequently in the North-east's habitual understatement. A North-east tourist might endure four hours of hurricane in Louisiana, in which thousands of homes are flattened and vehicles wrecked, and would phone home that night to report that: 'It's been a gey winnie day.'

Gie her a turnie
To try to entice a young woman at a dance. 'That's a rare bitta stuff (qv) ower in the back corner, Frederick. Awa ower and gie her a turnie.'

Gie him a clap wi a spade
A young woman being pestered by the amorous advances of a young man might turn to a third party and request such action.

Gies yer erse a nippie taste
Describes anything which is unpleasant. 'See that *Emmerdale Farm*; dis that programme nae gie yer erse a nippie taste?'

Gimmies
Gymshoes. 'Stop crying, Albert. The big boys flushing your gimmies down the toilet is no excuse for your PE kit being incomplete.' The G in Gimmies is pronounced as a J.

Ging
To go. 'Ging ower intae the corner and tak a run up yer humph.' (*I find you exasperating.*)

Ginge
Affectionate nickname for anyone with red hair. Pronounced as Jinj. 'Gaun oot the nicht, Ginge?'

Gink
Unattractive, unco-ordinated person, not very worldly. 'Fifteen and still plays wi his Lego. What a gink.' The G is hard.

Glae-eed
Ophthalmic flaw in which one eye is not aligned properly. 'She wis that glae-eed that ye wis nivver sure if she wis spikkin tae you or the wifie three seats back.' Also, there's a cornkister with the line: 'Ae ee says Forfar and the ither ee says Fife.'

Globie
Lightbulb. 'Pit in anither globie for me, wid ye? That een's blaan.' The poor durability and value of modern lightbulbs may then be emphasised with the codicil: 'It hisna laistit nae time.'

Gloryhole
No matter how exalted or modern the home, sooner or later it develops a gloryhole, the *room or cupboard where all the junk accumulates.* 'Mither, far wid the pliers be?' 'Try the gloryhole.'

Go
To hunger for. 'I could fair go a pyock o chips.'

Graip

Large garden fork of similar proportions to a spade. Believed to come from Norwegian, as so many Doric and Scots words do. This old word is still used by surprisingly young North-east Scots. A Banffshire head teacher told me of a primary schoolboy at a fishing-village pageant who had dressed as Neptune and was carrying an impressive home-made trident. When Neptune realised that he needed to go to the toilet, he looked round for a suitable custodian for the trident and, on picking a trustworthy adult, Neptune asked: 'I'm needin tae pee. Wid ye look efter ma graip?' Also, the *Press and Journal* once reported the court case of a man who had returned home early to discover his wife in flagrante delicto with the neighbour and who, in a touchingly North-east gesture, had run out to the garden shed, grabbed the garden fork and gone back to stab the lover several times. The newspaper's heading was: The Graip of Wrath. It was a pity that the wife hadn't later approached the paper to vent her anger about her graip-wielding husband, for the resulting feature could have been headed: 'The Gripes of Ruth.'

Grandie

Grand Central. One-time cinema in George Street, Aberdeen, whose heyday was marked by inexpensive showings of second-run features, but which, sadly, ended its days as a soft-porn venue for the dirty-mac brigade. Redeveloped in the 1980s as shops and flats, but the name lives on in a former church just round the corner which has been converted into a restaurant-pub, the Grandé.

Grannie's sookers

Large pandrops.

Greaseball

Anyone who is too smooth for his own good. 'See him? Thinks he's honey and the bees dinna ken. What a greaseball.'

Greetin match

A crying contest. Whenever children are growing tired or ill-tempered and their behaviour begins to worsen, sooner or later one or all will begin crying and fighting. That's a greetin match. 'Come on hame, Jim, afore the kids start a greetin match.' Nowadays, the phrase can also be used of a catfight between older women who ought to know better.

Grippy

Greedy. 'Ye widna get daylicht in a dark corner fae Chae. He's terrible grippy.' Contrary to popular myth, per head of population Aberdeen and the North-east consistently outstrip every other part of Scotland, bar Orkney and Shetland, for giving to charity. The philosophy is summed up best in the old Doric saying: 'It's nae loss fit a freen gets.' (What a friend gets is no loss.)

Growler

An extremely unattractive woman. 'Hiv ye seen oor Arthur's latest girlfriend? A richt growler.'

Grumpian

Grampian Television. The ITV contractor for North and East Scotland, founded in 1961, enjoys one of the highest ratings within its area of any ITV station. Now part of the Scottish Media Group, raising widespread fears that the North and North-east will be swamped by an advancing tide of Glaswegianism. However well the station does, it will always be referred to fondly by its core audience as 'Grumpian'. 'Turn ower and see fit's on Grumpian.' 'Grumpian hisna been the same since they did awa wi Jimmy Spunkie.'

Guffie

An Englishman or Englishwoman. The derivation is debated. The likeliest is that it was brought north by long-distance lorry-drivers, who were amused by their Cockney counterparts' habit of addressing everyone as 'guv', which became corrupted to 'guff'. A more modern explanation, given the immigration of so many of our southern cousins, is attributed to an English person's reputation for prattling excessively about nothing at all (guff) and for expressing

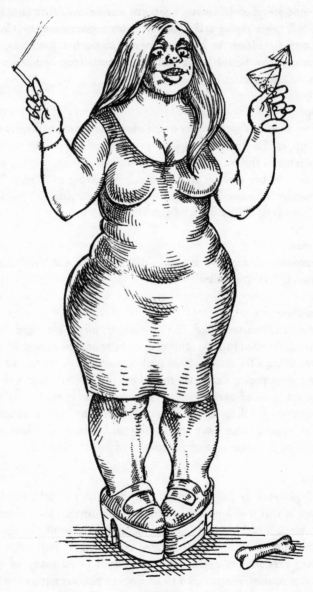

Growler

unsought opinions. 'There's that mony Guffies in Aiberdeenshire noo, the Doric's lik a breath o fresh air.' Also known as white settlers. One noted academic and son of the North-east once described a Guffie as 'someone who is unable to leave any silence unfilled'.

Guisin
Institutionalised begging in the run-up to November 5, whereby children knock at house doors seeking money to fund their Guy Fawkes fireworks.

Gull
See **Swick.**

Gulshach
Junk food. An all-purpose word to describe everything that is wrong in children's diet these days. Crisps are gulshach. Sweets are gulshach. Fizzy drinks are gulshach. 'I wid nivver interfere in ma dother-in-law's wye o bringin up her bairns, bit they get far ower muckle gulshach for my likin. They winna hae nae teeth by the time they leave the school.'

Gype
Idiot.

H

Haein on
Kidding. 'The Queen's holidayin in a caravan at the Broch? Ye're haein me on.'

Hakin
Searching. 'I've been hakin the Toon aa mornin for a frock for ma niece's weddin.'

Hale watter
The heaviest rain you can get. 'I widna ging ootside aenoo, Nessie. Nae even wi a brolly. It's hale watter.' Heavy rain can also be said to

be 'trippin ower itsel', 'comin doon lik stair-rods' and 'nae takkin its time'.

Half hung-tee
Lethargic. 'For ony sake, Arthur, ging tae yer bed a bittie earlier the nicht. Ye're stannin there half hung-tee.'

Halin aff
Pouring in torrents. Said mostly of perspiring humans. 'He spent twa oors hyowin neeps in the tap park in the blazin heat. The sweat wis jist halin aff him.'

Halved and quartered
Given a severe chastisement. 'If that grocer disna gie me ma siller back for that stinkin cheese he selt me, he'll be halved and quartered.'

Ham-and-egger
An incompetent person. 'I ken exactly fit's wrang wi this company. The hale place is filled wi ham-and-eggers.' Perhaps derives from the days when rank-and-file staff had to make do with brose and kail, while the bosses gorged themselves on ham and eggs. And we all know what rank-and-file staff think of bosses' competence.

Hard as Henderson's
Granite-hard. 'I've nivver eaten the wife's pastry. It's as hard as Henderson's.' Note that 'Henderson's' is pronounced 'Hinnerson's'. Great debate rages throughout the North-east as to the origin of this, and I'll be pleased to take advice. A slight majority holds that it comes from the old Aberdeen metalworks, Henderson's, whose products, as you would understand, were pretty hard. Others point to the variation 'as hard as Henderson's erse' as proof that the other theory is nonsense. Let me know.

Hashed
In a hurry. 'Canna stop for a news the day, Teenie. I'm affa hashed.'

Haud yer tongue

Be quiet. Any talkative person who has outstayed her welcome will be instructed thus sooner or later. Equally, someone who insists on paying the bill in a tearoom (a rare event) will be told by the others: 'Och, haud yer tongue, we'll aa pey wir share.'

Haudin thegither

Holding together. Reply to an inquiry after one's health. 'Foo are ye?' 'Och, haudin thegither.' Also **hingin thegither** or **hingin thegither bi a threid.**

Haud-up

Delay or *traffic jam.* 'Fit's aa the haud-up?' 'There's a Morris Minor went aff the road at Provost Rust Drive.'

Heaters

See **Cattie's faces.**

Heedrum-hodrums

Gaelic or Gaelic-speakers. 'I dinna ken fit Grumpian's thinkin aboot, pittin on aa that heedrum-hodrums a body canna mak oot.'

Heid and tail

In the days when big families were common and beds were hard to come by, children were required to sleep this way. Alternately, one child's head would be at the top of the bed, the next child's at the bottom, and so on and so forth, rather like sardines in a can, thus making maximum use of the bed width. People with cheesy feet must have been unpopular.

Heid bummer

The boss. 'Elsie's left her job. Couldna get on wi the heid bummer.'

Heid case

A deranged person. 'Kenny's a heid case at the best o times.' Known in parts of Aberdeen as a 'heid the ba'.

Heid o the road
A phrase used in describing anyone who can't or won't stay at home. 'Nae surprise her mairriage went doon the tubes; she wis nivver aff the heid o the road.'

Heppie's
Hepworth's the tailor. From the days when the national chain had a branch in seemingly every small town in the North-east. From discussions with those who patronised the stores, it seems that the chain's reputation was not what it might have been. Any local who was seen coming down the street stooping, limping or listing to starboard was popularly supposed not to have been injured, but simply to have had a new suit made up by Heppie's.

Here's yer hat, fit's yer hurry?
A phrase used as a means of getting rid of a visitor who has overstayed his welcome, without appearing to be rude. A host for whom this ploy does not work might consider turning up the heat with: 'The back o yer heid's a treat.'

Hin leg o a doo
Back leg of a pigeon. Meaning, non-existent or fabled. 'He says he's got a Rolls-Royce in a garage doon in Manchester, bit he says he canna let's see it because he's nae allowed tae tak it oot o England for the insurance. I think it's a hin leg o a doo, masel.' You can substitute the word **cushie** for doo.

Hine
Far. 'How far is Glasgow, my good fellow?' 'Oh, hine awa, hine awa.'

Hingin-luggit
Hang-eared, glum. 'Ye're terrible hingin-luggit, Gertie. Hiv ye lost a tanner and found a thripny?'

Hingin mince

Lank or dishevelled hair. 'Ye'd think Poppy wid hiv pit a brush through her hair afore she cam oot. It's lik hingin mince.'

Hinner eyn

The end or the tail. Tautologous description of the back end of anything. 'Eyn' would do perfectly well, but North-east people always refer to the hinner eyn. 'Oor Jason's got an important part in the school panto this year. He's the understudy for the hinner eyn o the horse.'

Hoatchin

Infested. 'No, ye canna play wi Billy Duncan. His heid's hoatchin wi lice.' Such a head might also be said to be **loupin**. There are two other meanings: a restless person could be said to be **hoatchin in his seat**. And a crowded place could be said to be **hoatchin wi fowk**, as in: 'Dinna look the road o Union Street ony Setterday afore Christmas; it'll jist be hoatchin'.

Hogmanay

December 31. Also a gift which is offered to celebrate the end of the year – frequently alcoholic, being the North-east. 'Ye'll jist come in and get yer Hogmanay, noo.' For children, their Hogmanay is a handout of smachrie (qv) and gulshach (qv), obtained by calling at house doors and reciting the old rhyme: 'Rise up, aul wife, and shak yer feathers, and dinna think that we are beggars. We're only bairnies oot tae play. Rise up and gie's wir Hogmanay.' The tradition is dying because (a) many parents do see it as begging and demeaning to their families, and (b) because of increasing fears for children's safety on dark nights. The same fears apply to Hallowe'en.

Homer

Any job of work which is executed outwith the normal tax regime. 'The boy next door put in wir fittit wardrobes. Fower hunder poun, plus materials, and ye'd nivver ken it wis a homer.' Derives from the fact that most of the work is carried out in homes, not offices or yards, or perhaps because the workman is based from his own home.

Hoatchin

Honk yer load

To be violently sick. 'She's hid vodka, gin, Bacardi, a coupla lager tops, Tequila, Crabbie's and a wee Cremola Foam. Nae surprise she honked her load in Belmont Street.'

Hoodjiecapiv

Banffshire equivalent of thingummyjig. Frequently shortened to 'hoodjie'. 'Could I hae a shottie o yer hoodjie?'

Horny golach

Earwig. See **Forkytail**. Earwig is the most common translation, but some communities in the hills seem to draw a distinction between a forkytail and a horny golach, which is a larger and more fearsome thing altogether, I'm told.

Horse intae

Consume enthusiastically. 'She went horsin intae that plate o stovies lik she'd nae seen maet for a month.'

Horsie-back

Rural version of Aberdeen's **coalie-back** (qv).

Howpie

A swig. 'Can I hae a howpie o yer ale?'

Howpie-up

A leg-up. 'You gie me a howpie-up and I'll gie you a howpie-up and we can baith hae a look through the changin-room windae. Deal?'

Hubber

A stutter or stammer. Not usually used cruelly or unfeelingly to describe a speech impediment, but more often to depict someone who is so excited that she is tripping over her words. 'Slow doon, Marigold; ye're hubberin.' In an engineering context, the word can also be used to describe an engine's note. A really experienced mechanic can listen intently to an engine as it runs and can offer an uncannily accurate diagnosis just by analysing 'the hubber'.

Hudderie
Scruffy. Can be used of anyone who is dressed badly or untidily, but is used most often nowadays of unruly hair that badly needs a visit to the salon. 'Hiv ye nae a caim, min? Ye're affa hudderie-heidit.'

Hummin a sweetie
Learning how to kiss. 'Hiv ye tried hummin a sweetie wi Izzie?' One partner would hold a large sweet between his teeth and offer the protruding part to his intended. If she accepted, their lips would brush.

Humph
A hump or hunchback. 'Peer Eb. He's got a humph lik a he ferret.' Anyone who stoops is said to be **humphy-backit**. See also **twa-faul**.

Hunger
Miser. The G is not pronounced hard as it is in the English word, but as in Hung. 'Say fit ye like aboot him, I maintain he's an affa hunger.'

Hut
Nothing to do with temporary buildings, but the past participle of the English verb 'to hit'. 'It wis Florrie's ain blame. She widna stan back fae the kerb like I said and fit happened? She got hut in the moo wi a bus mirror. She's nae lachin noo.' Occasionally, one can also be hutten. 'He got hutten on the back o the heid wi a cricket ba.'

Hytered
Tripped. 'She hytered ower a crackit slab and broke her airm.' Any spectacle in which a victim trips several times trying desperately to regain his balance between each one is said to be 'a hyter and styter'.

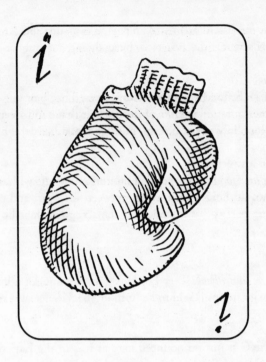

I

Icicle
Ice-lolly. North-east children don't eat ice-lollies. They eat icicles. These vary from the simplicity of the ice pole, which is more or less cordial frozen in a six-inch plastic tube, to the elaborate desserts on sticks dreamed up by Wall's and Lyons Maid. Whatever, they're all just icicles in the North-east. 'Mam, can I hae an icicle?' 'No, ye'll spile yer denner.'

Ill-fashioned
Nosy. 'They saw the furniture van ootside the hoose this mornin, and they were roon by wi a plate o new-made bannocks this aifterneen. They're the maist ill-fashioned pair I ivver cam across.'

Note: 'nosiness' is **ill-fashience**. 'They askit foo muckle I peyed for ma new BMW. Can ye believe the ill-fashience?'

Ill-natered
Foul-tempered. Can be ascribed to any age group, but is used most often of pensioners. 'Ye winna get yer ba back fae Aul Duguid. He widna gie a blin spurgie a worm. Terrible ill-natered.'

Ill-trickit
Mischievous. 'I wid watch that young loonie next door if I wis you. He's got an ill-trickit look aboot him.'

Intimmers
Insides. Derives from shipbuilding, in which the intimmers were the inward timbers of the hull. Now refers to the insides of everything from the human body to computers. 'I'd nae a wink o sleep last nicht, doctor. It's ma intimmers.' 'I canna mak heid nor tail o this new computer we've bocht. I screwed aff the lid, bit it's aa wires and silicon chips for intimmers.'

Inverted interrogative
A peculiar feature of Aberdonian grammar in which a statement has a rhetorical question tagged on to the end of the original sentence by means of a secondary clause. It is the question part which is given stress, viz: 'He's a handsome man, is he?' 'He wis richt good til his berrens, wis he?' 'She's jist Doon the Toon, is she?' The nearest translation to English form would be to convert the 'is he?', 'wis he?' and 'is she?' to 'isn't he?', 'wasn't he?' and 'isn't she?'.

Is *he* deid?
The curious and almost universal response to the news that so-and-so 'wis beeried last wikk'. The recipient of the news invariably adopts a surprised expression and asks: 'Is *he* deid?'

Ivnoo
See **Aenoo**.

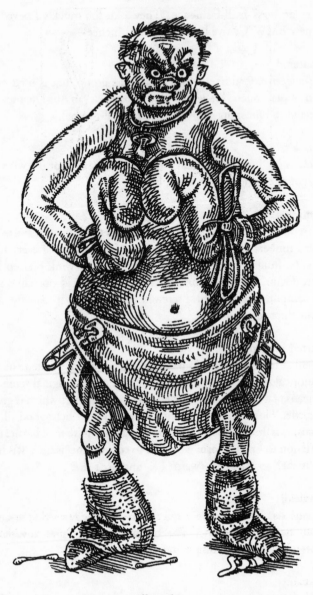

Ill-trickit

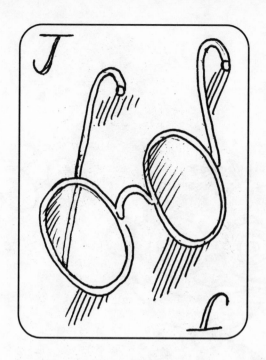

J

Jamaica
A furious tantrum. 'Could I bide at your hoose the nicht, Ally? If I ging hame in a state like this, the wife'll tak a Jamaica.' Origin uncertain.

Jammies
Pyjamas, but also extremely thick spectacles for the profoundly myopic. A contraction of 'jam-jar spectacles', presumably. 'Michty, I hardly kent ye, Wullie. That's affa jammies ye're weerin noo.'

Jing-bang
Whole lot. An expression not often found on its own. More often

Jammies

found with the word 'hale' as in 'hale jing-bang', meaning absolutely everything. 'I washed the team's fitba strip. They played ten minutes afore the game wis cried aff for bad weather, and I'd tae wash the hale jing-bang again.'

Joog
A jug. A small jug is a **joogie**. 'Awa doon til the diary and get's a joogie o cream, dearie.' There's also the celebrated exchange of two elderly North-east men discussing the legendary American songbird Tina Turner. 'I hear she's near sivventy.' 'Awaa, she's nivver sivventy. Nae jinkin aboot lik thon and weerin thon little short skirties that dinna hardly hap nithing.' 'I wyte she's sivventy. I read it in the paper. She gings hame at nicht in a wheelcheir, pits her wig in a box, her eyelashes in a draaer, her jewels in a safe, her sheen in a press, her breists in a joogie o warm watter and then they hing the rest o her up in a wardrobe.'

Jools
Jewellery. North-east women hardly ever refer to their adornments and trinkets as jewellery. They are almost always 'ma jools'.

Jotters
P45. 'I telt the boss he wis a big fat neep. Now I've got ma jotters.'

Juice
Fruit cordial. 'Can I hae a drink o juice, mam?' Older readers will recognise an alternative definition, being *the liquid or sauce in any tinned food.* 'I dinna like HP baked beans; there's nae enough beans and ower muckle juice.' 'Doreen likes tae drink the juice fae a tin o pineapple chunks.'

Jump yersel
Expression of exasperation. 'I'm fed up argying wi ye. Awa and jump yersel.' Equally: 'Awa and tak a lang jump.'

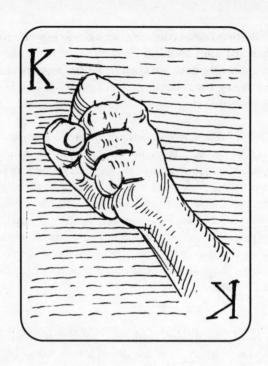

K

Keek

Sneaky peek. Comes from the Dutch word 'kijk', meaning look. 'Tak a keek roon the corner and see fit that twa's up til.' A black eye is known as a **keeker**.

Ken?

Do you know? For some obscure reason, this is applied as an interrogative suffix to an Aberdonian's conversational sentences whether it belongs there or not. 'I went oot tae the bingo, ken? I won twinty poun for a tap line, ken? We got a taxi hame, ken? Ma man wis lyin sleepin on the settee, ken?'

Ken ee fa that is? Deil the ken. Ken ee, ken I, ken ony o's? Steer the porritch or I hae a look.

Complete gibberish, said supposedly by a group of Lumsden women on spying a stranger in their village. What earthly good it did them, I haven't a clue.

Ken fine

Know perfectly well. 'Ye ken fine fit I mean, so dinna gie me ony o yer Mr Wide-eyed and Innocent.'

Kennel

An off-the-shelf timber-framed house. 'I see that's anither kennel gaun up at the end o the village.'

Kickin

Physical assault. 'That young lad's oot o control. Somebody'll gie him a richt kickin een o this nichts and he'll deserve it.' That's the Aberdeen word. The rural word is **gyan-ower**. Note that while a gyan-ower is a physical assault, an **ower-gyan** is purely verbal. 'What an ower-gyan I got fae ma boss this aifterneen.'

Killer

A gargantuan meal. Also known as a **tightener**. Killer derives from the old Scots phrase: 'He looks lik a gweed plate o mince wid kill him.'

Kindlers

Kindling sticks. 'Awa ootside and hack a puckle kindlers for the morn's fire.'

King Lear

A dreamer or hopeless fantasist. The North-east's version of Walter Mitty or Billy Liar is name because the Doric word for a liar is pronounced 'lee-ar', so the most accomplished liar of all is the King Lee-ar.

Kniv

Kink hoast

Originally whooping cough, but now any particularly hacking cough. Kink comes, presumably, from kinkit, meaning doubled up. 'Michty Charlie, ye winna be lang wi's; ye're terrible wi the kink hoast.'

Kinker

Kincardine O'Neil. 'Are ye gaun til the dunce at the Kinker on Setterday?' Coincidentally, Kincardine O'Neil is famous still as the victim of one of the worst commercial decisions of the 19th century. The local laird refused to allow the Deeside railway through his land. Consequently, the line snaked away on a wide loop north, through Torphins and Lumphanan to give Kincardine O'Neil a wide berth. It was the making of those two villages, while Kinker, the oldest and once one of the busiest and most important communities along Deeside, slipped into more than a century of decline. Only now, with the growth of commuter traffic, is it recovering.

Kinnell

A small explosion, although used most commonly of excessive gastric wind. Stress the second syllable. 'They're blastin at Kemnay Quarry again. What a kinnell there wis this mornin.' Can also be used as a verb, hence: 'Will ye stop that kinnellin or get oot o the car?'

Kirk or a mill o't

A church or a mill of it. If it's not one thing, it's the other. 'Jackie's a fine boy, bit he aye maks a kirk or a mill o't.'

Kittlins

Kittens, but also *small children.* 'Kittlins shouldna be oot that late. It's a winder that femly's nae reportit.'

Kniv

Fist. The K is silent. 'Tak that bak or ye'll taste ma kniv.' Note: when a father is teaching his young son how to look after himself in a playground fight, the first lesson involves teaching the boy to 'mak a kniv'.

Knot

Not something you study in the Boy Scouts, but simply *a lump in any food which should be smooth*. Pronounce both K and N. 'I canna aet ma mither's custard; it's fulla k-nots.' Flaws in timber are also k-nots.

Knotty Tams

An oatmeal dish that is similar to brose (qv), but made with milk instead of water.

Knype

To hurry. Pronounce both K and N. 'Bob's surely gaun oot wi his lass the nicht. He's knypin doon the road wi his tongue hingin oot.' One form of the word can also be used as a response to the inquiry: 'Foo are ye deein?' 'Ach, aye knypin on.'

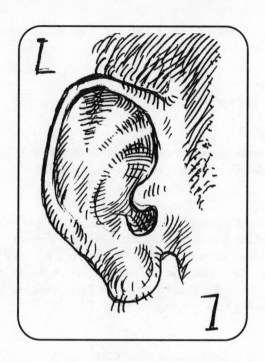

L

Lager tops
Lager with a dash of lemonade added. The dash (or **skite** (qv)) is only enough to give the drink a refreshing taste, but not so much as to make it sickly.

Lang stan
A long stand. A joke played on probably every apprentice who has served his time in the North-east, whereby the foreman would instruct the new recruit to go to the storeman and ask for 'a lang stan'. The storeman would listen to the request and then leave the lad standing in the corner for half an hour or more – a lang stan –

until the boy realised he had been had. A variation was to be sent for a tin of tartan paint.

Lavvie-diver
Slang term for a plumber.

Legoland
Any new estate of timber-framed houses, which are increasingly common on the edges of many North-east towns and villages.

Licks
Punishment. Despite protracted inquiries, I can't get a definitive answer for the derivation of this, but North-east children who have been punished are said to have been 'gien their licks'. I'll happily take advice. 'Pit doon that pentbrush and come awa fae the new carpet, Felicity, or yer dad'll gie ye yer licks.' One can also give something **big licks**, meaning to put in a lot of effort.

Lirks
Midriff rolls of fat showing through the clothing. 'June weers terrible ticht brikks and ticht tops. Ye can hardly see her for lirks.' 'Ay, June's fairly burstin out all over.'

Loafers
Aberdeen name for mixed boiled sweets. 'Sees a quarter o loafers, grocer. We're awa til the fillims.'

Lodge Walk
The name still used by older Aberdonians for the city's police HQ, so called because of its proximity to an old Aberdeen lane of that name. Lodge Walk has long since been supplanted by the nearby Queen Street HQ, a towering homage to 1960s architecture, but the old name persists. This explains the notorious story in 1970s Aberdeen about one city notable who was known to have a thing about men in police uniform and who was not shy of sharing her

affections if the opportunity arose. Her colleagues, who disapproved of so cosy a liaison with the bobbies, were often heard to remark that 'there's mair fingerprints on that wifie than there is in the Lodge Walk files'. Pardon me for lowering the tone, but I'm only the messenger.

Loon
A boy. Strictly speaking, a loon is unmarried, but most North-east men are loons from birth to death. 'Ye're an affa loon, granda.'

Low door
Bottom-floor flat in a tenement. A prized council let, supposedly reserved for older tenants. 'I wis winderin, cooncillor, if ye could get ma mither a low door.'

Lucky bag
Type of children's confectionery. This was a sealed paper bag (which cost 3d in the mid-1960s) containing half a dozen small, cheap sweets, a motto and a cheap plastic toy that broke on the first attempt to play with it, or which was pretty pointless in any case. Children soon learned that lucky bags were poor value. Perhaps this explains the common insult which is still employed whenever someone seeks to poke fun at another person's new purchase. 'Rare car, Tam. Did ye get it in a lucky bag?'

Lugs
Ears, obviously. Anyone with particularly prominent or protruding examples is said to have 'lugs lik pot hunnles' (ears like pot handles). Such prominent ears are also described as **flappers**.

Lugs-be-buggered
Nickname for anyone with prominent ears. 'Awa ower and see fit Lugs-be-buggered wints tae drink.'

Lumpie
The Blue Lamp public house in Gallowgate, Aberdeen. Age-old

Lugs

popular tavern, now frequented by a high proportion of students from nearby universities. 'I'll see ye at the Lumpie at half-nine.'

Lundies
Skipping-rope game in which two people spin two long ropes at once and a third child does the skipping. 'We've got ae rope already. If you wid gie's a shot o yours, we could aa play lundies.'

M

Ma's
Cameron's public house. One of the oldest (and busiest) taverns in Scotland. It's in Little Belmont Street, Aberdeen. Although the snug bar at the front is small and, on busy nights, extremely cramped, its aficionados declare stoutly that no other bar in Aberdeen matches it for atmosphere. There's a large lounge at the back now, in any case. Ma Cameron's was long since abbreviated to Ma's. 'We'll dee the rounds and finish at Ma's.'

Madam Murray's
Celebrated school of dance in Aberdeen. Most Aberdonians over 50

wax lyrical about Madam Murray's, for this was where most of them learned the quickstep, waltz and sundry other terpsichorean manoeuvres.

Magic Roundabout
CB-radio nickname for Huntly. So called because of the large roundabout which appeared on the town's southern edge when it was bypassed by the A96. Others include Sawmill City (Elgin).

Mahogany
A haircut that is cropped as closely as possible without actually being a shave. 'Foo muckle aff the day, sir?' 'Doon tae the mahogany.' A similar phrase would be **intae the quick**, which comes from someone who bites her nails so voraciously that there is virtually no nail left.

Makkin on
Pretending. 'See him ower there flashin fivers, makkin on he's weel-aff.' Not to be confused with . . .

Makkin on
Fondling. A common charge in the days when kirk sessions heard and punished the misdemeanours of hot-blooded parishioners. Guilty parties were noted in the session minutes as 'fornicator and fornicatrix, lying abed and makkin on'.

Mangled
See **Minced**.

Mappie
A rabbit or, in some parts of Banffshire and Buchan, a temper tantrum. 'Mappies hiv aeten a' ma man's lettuce. What a mappie he took.' **Mappie-moos** are antirrhinums, so called because they look like a rabbit's mouth and if the flower heads are squeezed, they quiver like a sniffing rabbit.

Mappie

Mattie

Any maternity unit, but usually Aberdeen Maternity Hospital. 'Quick, officer, the Mattie afore it's ower late.'

Mealie jimmie

White pudding. A six-inch mélange of oatmeal, onion, lard and spices, forced into an edible skin, covered in batter and deep fried. Yet another feature in the North-east Scotland healthy eating repertoire, but delicious all the same. When served with chips, it becomes, in chipper parlance, 'a fite-poodin supper'. Connoisseurs have been known to bypass several perfectly good chippers and travel many miles to reach the establishment which, in their judgment, serves the finest examples. I have been inconsolable since the Northern Fish Bar at Huntly shut down. The best mealie jimmies are moist and cloying when cooked or, as we say, 'sappy'. Some people refer to mealie jimmies as mealie jerkers.

Meen

The moon. A common male exclamation when spying a woman bending over is: 'I see the meen's oot.' An amply upholstered example might earn: 'I see the meen's oot. And it's full.' (Pronounced as in hull). Also, the moon's last quarter is noted by: 'The meen's on her back.' Some older North-easters take seeing this as a sign of bad weather.

Messages

The shopping. 'Awa and dee the messages for yer mam, dearie.' Also known as **eerans** (errands). The receptacle in which the shopping is carried is the **message-bag**.

Milesteen inspector

An idler. The North-east's version of lead-swinger. Derives from a lazy person's habit of filling his days by strolling the highways and by-ways.

Min

All-purpose form of address to any male individual. This is the Doric form of 'my good man', I suppose. 'Hey, min; stop kickin that cat.' 'Awa hame til yer bed, min.' 'Fit like the day, min?'

Minced

Drunk almost to the point of unconsciousness. The worrying thing is that this comes from listening to schoolchildren, who were heard recounting a splendid social occasion one previous Friday night in which most of their contemporaries 'wis minced'. Also in regular use are **Mirack** (short for **miraculous**), **Stottin**, **Guttered**, **Bladdered**, **Blootered**, **Blitzed**, **Mashed**, **Lummed**, **Slaughtered**, **Roarin**, **Rubber-leggit**, **Wastit**, **Wrecked** and **Deein the Alky Twostep**. The number of North-east synonyms for alcoholic abandon is truly wondrous.

Minker(s)

Person or persons of low social standing. 'That's an affa collection o minkers that's moved in at number twinty-three.'

Mischanter

Mishap or accident. The C is silent. 'Dinna be angry, Wullie, bit I've hid a bit o a mischanter in the car. There's watter in the manifold.' 'Far aboot is it?' 'In the herber.'

Miss That Hisna Been Missed

A single woman who has known an excess of physical pleasures. 'Nae muckle winner Hilda's past her best at forty. She's a miss that hisna been missed.' Equally: 'She hisna been neglectit.'

Mochie

Grey, dreary. Hence the old joke about Noah and the ark enduring 40 days and nights of storms and finally spotting a little outcrop of rock, little realising that it is the very top of Bennachie. They sail closer and, peering through driving rain, realise that someone is perched thereon. As they draw even closer, they see Wullie, a North-east farmworker, who hails them with a friendly wave and shouts: 'Ay-ay, Noah. Mochie day.'

Modeller
Model Lodging House, East North Street, Aberdeen. One-time hostel for gentlemen of the road, closed in the early 1990s. 'I'm nae parkin in East North Street; it's ower close tae the Modeller for my likin.'

Mollach
To hang around or be idle. 'Are you still mollachin inside on a bonnie day like this?' It might derive from the habits of the mole; who knows?

Monkey Hoose
Building on the corner of Union Terrace and Union Street, Aberdeen, where courting couples would meet before going on elsewhere. The name could come from one of two sources. There might have been a monkey design on the tall cast-iron railings or, more likely, people sheltering under the portico and behind the railings would peer out at the darkening skies and would seem, to passers-by, like monkeys in a cage at the zoo.

Mooch
To beg or borrow. 'She wis roon moochin a cuppa sugar this mornin and me nae even oot o ma goon.' Such a person is said to be 'on the mooch' or 'on the tap'.

The morn
Tomorrow. 'Come ower for yer denner the morn.' 'I'll pick ye up at echt the morn's mornin.' 'Pit on yer party frock and we'll ging oot clubbin the morn's nicht.'

MoT
Regular check on any car over three years old, but also the recommended health check on any woman over a certain age. 'I'm awa doon tae the surgery for ma MoT. I hope she waarms her haans.'

Mutant Alley
Taxi-drivers' nickname for Windmill Brae, Aberdeen, one-time hub of the early-morning clubbing set who appear to favour copious vomiting in gutters and, in their cups, picking fights with passing cars. Only brave taxi-drivers venture down Mutant Alley. If you happen to take a wrong turning after midnight on any Friday or Saturday and find yourselves therein, stick to the taxi-drivers' golden rule: 'No eye contact'.

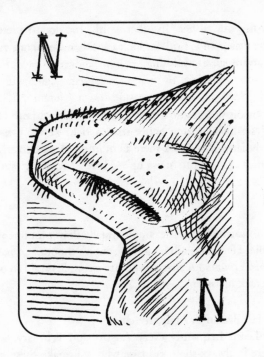

N

Nae handy
Idiomatic and, thus, impossible to translate accurately. Used at the end of a spoken sentence when the speaker is trying to lay extra stress. 'I went doon til the cat and dog home. There wis barkin and myowin nae handy.' Or: 'She won twa thoosan at the bingo last nicht. She wis in a state nae handy.'

Nae sair
Not painful. Anyone who is told that her grey hair is beginning to show will reply: 'It's nae sair.'

Nae side
Describing someone who is open and honest. 'Say fit ye like aboot Ina,

bit there's nae side til her.' In other words, Ina doesn't present one face to one group and another face to another. She treats everyone the same and is admired for it.

News
A noun, obviously, but also a verb in the North-east, both meaning *gossip*. 'Mysie likes nithing better than a richt news.' Or: 'Dinna news wi Mysie; ye'll be stuck there aa mornin.' A particularly vigorous practitioner is said to 'news up': 'There's Mysie, newsin up the postie.'

Nib
Nose. An unusually lustrous example usually draws comment, as in: 'Peer Wullie. He's got a nib lik a blin souter's thoom.' (*A nose like a blind cobbler's thumb.*) A sharp or pointy example is said to be 'a nib that wid crack hailsteens'.

Nichts is fair draain in / fair stretchin
A phrase heard frequently every August and February. In every circle, there is always some sad case who will make these observations on June 23 and December 23. Just humour him.

Nickum
A mischievous young boy; not quite a hooligan. 'I widna say her loonie's richt coorse; he's mair o a nickum.'

Nip
Dram. Not only does it mean a shot of whisky, 'nip' is a marvellous all-purpose word in North-east Scotland. To **nip on** is to crack along at a brisk pace. To have a **nippit tongue** is to be curt. One can be **nippit**, as in caught red-handed (nippit for speedin). And any physical space can be **nippit**, as in confined.

Nippie
A waitress. 'Shout ower the nippie and get her tae gie this table a

100

Nib

dicht.' Derives, presumably, from the necessity for any waitress to be quick on her feet.

Nippie sweeties
Describing anyone who is sour or uncharitable. 'The aul boy at number sivventeen's nippy sweeties and nae mistake.'

Nivver a bad that couldna be waur
Doric at its most fatalistic. *Nothing is so bad that it can't get worse.* Or, to put it another way: 'When one door shuts, another one slams in your face.'

Nivver dee't a winter yet
You haven't died in any winter so far. Said to anyone who is complaining about freezing cold, because they are obviously still alive despite the chill. 'Ye're caul? Ye've nivver dee't a winter yet. Now, I mind the winter o forty-sivven . . .'

North-east man
Once a regular character in the pages of the *Press and Journal,* leading to headings such as 'North-east man wins Olympic gold.' 'North-east man saves hundreds in Peru landslide.' 'North-east man to head Government task force.' 'North-east man wins millions in Mongolian lottery.' He fairly got about, North-east man. Note that the scurrilous rumour that the *Daily Journal's* heading on the morning of the *Titanic* sinking was 'North-east man lost at sea' is fiction.

Nott
Needed. 'Ye'd better finish yer dram, Geordie. That's yer wife on the phone. She says ye've visitors and ye're nott at hame.'

Nowt
Cattle. 'That's a bonnie park o nowt ye hiv there, Mains.' An alternative is **beasts**.

Yer number's nae dry

Snapped at any young blade with opinions beyond his years, knowledge or experience. Comes from the days of National Service, when a raw recruit was so new that his service number had only just been inscribed. 'Be quaet, min. Ye dinna ken fit ye're spikkin aboot. Yer number's nae dry yet.' Alternatively: 'Ye're nae lang oot o hippens.' *(It wasn't so long ago that you were still wearing nappies.)*

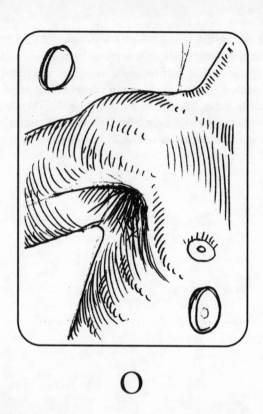

O

Oatmeal monument
An unusually useless or accident-prone person. The North-east version of chocolate teapot or motorbike ashtray. 'Far did ye get that new office loon? He's a big oatmeal monument.'

Ogie-pogies
Sweets similar to gobstoppers, which changed colour as they dissolved. No longer sold, unfortunately, but remembered fondly among those aged 50 or over, who still refer to any large sweet which any normal mouth can barely accommodate as an ogie-pogie.

On the turn
Soft in the head. 'She's got a spleet-new washin machine, bit she still

gaes doon tae the burnie and washes oot her draaers on a steen. On the turn, if ye ask me.'

One-drapper
An interment. From the patois of long-distance lorry-drivers, in which a one-drapper (one-delivery trip) was a prized load because the entire contents of the lorry could be offloaded at one point, instead of in time-consuming bits and pieces here and there. The 'big one-drapper' is one's final meeting with one's maker.

Oot o langour
Occupied and productive. 'Spent the hale mornin in yer gairden, Gordon? Ach, weel, it's kept ye oot o langour.'

Orra
Ragged or *distasteful.* In some parts of Aberdeenshire, the pronunciation is 'ory'. 'The wye some young lassies dresses up for the school nooadays is richt orra.' In old farming times, the **orraloon** was the young lad on the farm who did all the jobs no one else wanted, or had the time, to tackle.

Orra breet
Foul-mouthed person. 'Ye canna tak Mary onywye; she's sic an orra breet.'

Ower the heid
Completely submerged. Said mostly of water, but can be used of other things, as in: 'Nae bingo the nicht, Annie. I'm ower the heid wi ironin.'

The best ower-the-heid story comes from a retired nurse at Huntly, whose ward sister at Aberdeen Royal Infirmary in the 1930s was a harridan. One evening, an old chap had been knocked into Aberdeen Harbour and had almost drowned. Luckily, he was fished out in time and taken to hospital.

When sister was doing the rounds next morning, she came to the old chap's bed.

Oxters

'Well, my man,' she said imperiously. 'I hear that last night you were immersed in water.'

'Ma erse in watter?' he said. 'I wis ower the bliddy heid in watter.'

Ower the pailin
A mid-morning chat between neighbours. So-called because the women of neighbouring houses would pause in their housework duties and each take a cup of tea out to the back doorstep and converse across the mutual fence (pailin). 'That's the dustin finished. I'll awa for an ower-the-pailin wi Betty.'

Oxters
Armpits. 'Pit a skite o something roon yer oxters, Robert; they're singin (qv).' 'She ran intae the midden and wis up til her oxters in sharn.' An **oxter-staff** is a crutch. An **oxter-up** is a cuddle.

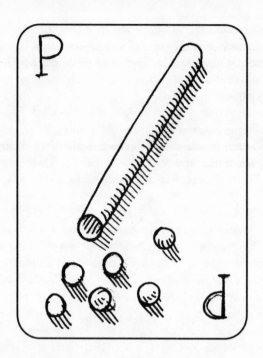

P

Paila watter

Pail of water. A towering insult used as the coup de grâce in an argument between two Aberdeen tenement housewives. As one woman sensed impasse approaching, she would begin to turn on her heels and, departing, would deliver her knockout blow: 'Awa and fling a paila watter roon that hoose o yours.' The implication is that the other party's standards of housewifery are not up to much.

Panjoteralised

Blind-drunk. A word made popular by the late Jaikie Stuart, of Ellon. 'I doot Erchie winna be up early the day; he wis fair panjoteralised last nicht.'

Pan-loff
A particular style of bread popular throughout most of Scotland, but also the habit of speaking BBC English when you have not been raised to it. To behave thus is described, rather dismissively, as 'to pan-loff it'. See also **Doon throwe it.**

Pannie
Saucepan and/or its contents. 'Ye'll jist come roon for yer denner. I've on a pannie o mince.'

Parcel
A mailed package, obviously, but also a well-filled nappy. 'Tak that parcel oot o the hoose and burn it, for ony sake.'

Peter Dick
A playing card inserted between the spokes of a pushbike in such a way as to produce a roaring noise in direct proportion to the speed of the bike. A favourite of boys between the wars. Anyone who wants to know how the name arose should fit up a bike as described and try riding it as slowly as possible. Listen to the sound. It's also a musical instrument, made from a small plank of wood with a thumb-board tied with string. It's played usually to give two or three short beats followed by one long one.

Peter's Thoom
One of the black marks behind the gills of a haddock, supposed to be the fingerprints of St Peter.

Pey the factor
Defecate. Comes from the days when the only reason any farm servant would be allowed to take a break from labour in the fields was to go and pay his rent. 'Peyin the factor' became a handy excuse for anyone who needed a bowel movement in a hurry. 'If ye'll excuse me, I'd better awa and pey the factor.' The phrase is still used by people who wouldn't know a factor or a plooed park if they fell over one.

Photie

Photograph. 'That wis a super photie o Finlay in the daily the day.' Equally, anyone who has been staring at an individual for too long might be asked somewhat brusquely: 'Div ye wint a photie?'

Pints

Not an imperial measure of volume, but simply shoelaces. One is admonished to tie up one's laces with the phrase: 'Dee up yer pints.' If one's laces have come undone, the friendly warning is: 'Hey, min; yer pints is louse.'

Pirn-taed

Stance in which the front of each foot points towards the other. 'The last time I saw something as pirn-taed as that, it wis clockin in a fairm close and layin eggs.' Also, **bow-hoched** means bandy-legged.

Pirr

Banffshire-coast expression for angry distress. 'The furniture van cam wi her new sofa and the airms wis torn. She got hersel in a richt pirr.'

Pit in

To plant. No one plants anything in a North-east garden. We 'pit in'. 'I've pit in twa dreel (qv) o Kerr's pinks this 'ear.' 'Fit kinna carrots are ye pittin in this 'ear, Dode?'

Pit on

Airs and graces. 'I dinna ken fit wye Wilma hauds sic a pit-on. Her faither wis jist a barber.' Also, **pit by** (to lay aside), as in: 'Ina's pittin by for her waddin. It'll nivver happen.' **Pit tee** (to add), as in: 'Is there a collection gaun roon for Harry? I'll pit tee twa poun.' And **sair pit-on**, a noun meaning ill. 'I'm affa sair pit-on wi the flu.'

Pit ye aff deein

Put you off dying, describing something which is so thoroughly depress-

ing that it's more depressing than the prospect of death itself. 'Nae anither episode o *EastEnders*, for ony sake. That mob o Cockney whiners wid pit ye aff deein.'

Pixie
Cheap rainhood. 'That's it startit spittin. Could ye len's a pixie?'

Pizzers
Peasemeal brose (qv).

Pizzies
A particular size of marble for school-playground games. Among other marble (bool) sizes were glaissers, picks and steelers.

Plenty watter
Anyone who is being offered water for his whisky will be asked how much water he likes in his dram. The standard reply is: 'Half and half, plenty watter', implying that plenty whisky is required, too.

Plottin
Not scheming but *flushed and sweating.* This Aberdeen City word is heard usually on hot or close (humid) days, the customary cry being 'I'm fair plottin.'

Pluffer
Originally the barrel of a bicycle-pump or a hollow stalk of cow parsley (not giant hogweed, which is dangerous) down which roddens (rowanberries) were propelled by mouth power. Nowadays any peashooter. 'No, ye canna buy a pluffer. Ye'll tak somebody's ee oot.'

Plunkit
Hidden. 'I've plunkit the loon's Christmas at the back o the wardrobe. He'll likely find it fitivver.'

111

Pluffer

Pluntit
Planted. Used in not particularly respectful circles to report a burial. 'Aul Tam wis pluntit last wikk.'

Poggit
Stuffed. Derivation unknown, but the word is used usually of some-one who has eaten too much, as in: 'Look at grunnie sleepin aff her Christmas denner aneth the tree. Fair poggit.'

Pollute
Polite. Said in order to pull the leg of someone who is doing their level best not to use slang in company. 'Mercy, Alistair, you're being awful pollute the day.' The famous story concerns the woman who was trying to explain to her posh friends why her dress was so muddy: 'On the way here, I trippit over a tree trunk and fell sklyte among the dibs.'

Pooch
Pocket. It's often said of a grippy person that he has 'lang pooches and short airms'.

Poochie
A segment of an orange or tangerine. 'See's anither poochie o yer orange, granda.' Sometimes known as **a pappie**.

Poshie
Child's name for porridge.

Pottie
Child's po, of course, but also window putty. A celebrated Aberdeen joinery firm was known throughout the city simply as Pottie Donald's, hence the cry whenever anyone bought an old banger in the 1960s, only to discover that its rusting bodywork had been repaired with copious amounts of filler covered by a sly lick of paint, that 'This Anglia's got mair pottie than Pottie Donald's yard.'

Potties

Nickname for Potarch, tiny settlement at a crossing over the River Dee between Banchory and Aboyne. Long a favourite destination for a Sunday run, a dip in the river, a read of the *Sunday Post* and a snooze with the car window wound down.

Preenicks

Small pins, but more usually the needles on evergreen trees. 'That's the last time I buy a Christmas tree fae a mannie at the pub. It wisna even Christmas Eve and the livin-room wis knee-deep in preenicks.'

Press

A cupboard. Nothing to do with the Fourth Estate. 'Pit that dizzen eggs on the tap shelf in the press.'

Prig

Not a self-important moralist but a verb meaning *to plead or entreat.* It's used most often in the negative in the North-east, as in: 'If he disna wint tae dee't, I'm nae wastin ma time priggin wi him.'

Pu

Pull. Pronounced 'poo'. 'Awa and pu some carrots for the broth.'

Puddle-louper

Any small jalopy deemed barely able to negotiate a puddle. 'Thon car-salesman saw oor Sammy comin. What a puddle-louper he's bocht.'

Puddocks' eggs

Frogs' eggs. Tapioca pudding. Also known as **birdies' een** (*birds' eyes*).

Pyock

A small bag. 'I'll hae a bottle o ale and a pyock o chips.'

Q

Queerin

Gizzard of any poultry. 'Mina, clean twa hens and tak them doon tae Mrs Duncan; she's nae feelin hersel. And mind and tak oot the queerin.'

Queets

Ankles. 'That's a fine pair o queets ye hiv there, Nellie. Are ye deein onything the morn's nicht?' One may also go ower ma queet(s) sprain one's ankle(s). 'I wid certainly come up a Gay Gordons wi ye, bit I went ower ma queets in the Dashin Fite Sergeant.'

Quine

A female person. Comes from 'queen', I suppose. Strictly speaking, a quine is unmarried, but many older, married women are referred to as quines as a gentle form of flattery. 'Fit like the day, quine?' A really young girl is 'a quinie'. 'Peer little quinie canna find her mither.'

R

Rabat

To rebel. 'I've tried dressin oor Sandra in bonnie frocks, but she jist rabats.'

Raffled

Anyone who disapproves of another's actions, proposals or ideas would urge them: 'Awa and get raffled.' 'Six thoosan for an aul banger lik that? Awa and get raffled.'

Raggie Morrison's

Former drapery in St Nicholas Street, Aberdeen, revered for the breadth of its stock and its keen pricing. The site has been occupied by the

Marks and Spencer store for 40 years. 'Awa doon tae Raggie's. I bet they'll hae jist fit ye're efter.'

Rakin
See **Hakin**.

Ran-dan
A night on the town. 'Ye're affa toffed-up, quines. Awa oot on the ran-dan?'

Rare
Adjective to describe anything which is deemed excellent. 'That's a rare new coat ye've got, Madge.' 'That's a rare shine ye've got on yer car, Eric.'

Rare spikker
Eloquent orator. 'The trouble wi politics nooadays is that they hinna the rare spikkers they eese't tae hae.' A precocious child who is able to form sentences well ahead of age can also be said to be 'a rare spikker'.

Rax
To reach, stretch or *strain.* 'Rax ower the table and get's the saut.' 'I spent the hale day hackin kindlers and noo I've raxed ma back.'

Redd yer crap
Literally, *tidy your crop.* An ornithological encouragement to get things off your chest.

Redd-up
A mess and, curiously, also *to tidy up a mess.* 'Maxine, yer bedroom's a helluva redd-up. Sort it oot now or I'll come and gie it a redd-up masel.'

Returned unopened
Often said of a lady who is free with her favours: 'Hilda's oot ilky nicht and nivver returned unopened.'

Rift

Bring up wind. 'If I eat even ae slice o cucumber I'll be riftin aa nicht.'

Riggit

Dressed to a presentable standard. 'Let me see. Hunkie. Comb. Tie's straicht. Sheen's polished. Yes, petal, that's me riggit.'

Rikkin

Exuding smoke. Comes probably from the German verb 'rauchen', to smoke. Rikkin can also be used to describe someone who is barely controlling her anger. 'Be real careful fit ye say tae Jessie. I saw her five minutes syne and she's rikkin.' Anything which has suffered smoke damage is said to be **rikkit**. An inhabited house is **a rikkin lum**. Anyone who is in his cups is said to be **rikkin o drink**.

Roadit

Fully prepared. Derives from someone being set to begin a journey or, in other words, to take to the road. 'Let me see. Passport, tickets, travellers' cheques — ay, that's me roadit.' Anyone who is **roadit again** has recovered from illness.

Rolie

Home-made cigarette. 'A packet o Rizlas and a box o spunks, please. I'm on the rolies noo.'

Rome and Spain

Stay-at-home holiday. Explained best by the customary exchange: 'Are ye gaun onywye for yer hol'days this summer?' 'Jist Rome and Spain. I'll Rome Aiberdeen and Spain aa ma siller.'

Row

To wrap. The OW is pronounced as in Cow. 'Dinna buy dear paper for rowin up Christmas parcels. It jist gets torn aff and flung oot.' Note that a row (a line) of anything in Doric is a **raw**. Unless it's vegetables, in which case it's a **dreel** (qv). Not much wonder incomers get confused.

Rift

Rowie
See **Buttery**.

Runnie
A recreational trip in the car, usually with two couples and usually undertaken on a Sunday afternoon. Something of a North-east social phenomenon. 'Come on and we'll awa for a runnie up Deeside. We'll maybe stop for a slider at Potties (qv).'

Runtit
Flat broke. A corruption of the English word 'runted', meaning 'made the runt of the litter'. 'I took ma girlfriend oot for a meal on Friday, then we went tae the picters and finished aff at a club. That wis me runtit for a fortnicht.'

The Rural
Scottish Women's Rural Institute. Linchpin of community life for many countrywomen, hence the cry: 'That's me awa til the Rural. I've markit the bottle.'

Rushed
Overcharged. 'Foo muckle wis ye rushed for yer new kitchen?'

S

Sair erse
A habitual complainer. 'Dinna bother listenin tae Betty. She's a richt sair erse.'

Sair haun
Sore hand. Anyone walking and eating something at the same time is said to have a sair haun. Derivation unknown, but perhaps something to do with the fact that a jam sandwich of white bread looks like blood seeping through a bandage. Alternatively, it might have something to do with the way a bandaged hand must be held up to avoid painful contact with anything else.

Sair heidie
Small cake. Peculiar to family bakers in the North-east, this was a queen-cake mixture wrapped with a band of greaseproof paper or rice paper. The result looked like a bandaged head, hence its popular name.

Sair-made
Pained. 'Fit's adee (qv) wi ye the day? Ye're walkin affa sair-made.'

Salad
Never mind rocket, basil, vinaigrette, mayonnaise, Dijon mustard or any other fancy or foreign muck. A salad in the North-east is always a lettuce leaf, two halves of tomato, a slice of biled ham, two slices of Baxter's pickled beetroot, half a boiled egg and, if it's Sunday, a slap of Heinz salad cream. Now eat that and be thankful; there are bairnies in Africa that would be delighted.

Saps
A bowl of bread or buns soaked in warm milk. Staple diet of many a toothless pensioner even as late as the 1960s. Might even still be a dish favoured in private, curtains drawn, among consenting adults who are labouring with troublesome dentures and raw gums.

Sclabdadder
Any item of excessive size, but usually food. 'Mercy, Tam; that's an affa sclabdadder o a bradie in yer piecebox the day.'

Sclap
A word which evokes very effectively the sound of someone falling headfirst into mud. 'She hytered and stytered and fell sclap amon dubs (mud).'

Scoff
That which is eaten. Also, *to eat.* Hence: 'Fit are ye haein for the scoff the nicht, Davie? A pan o stovies? Michty, ye'll seen scoff that.'

Sconed dock
Heated backside. Used in more polite company than its sister expression, **skelpit erse**, hence: 'Come inside this minute, Alistair, or it's a sconed dock for you, young man.'

Scottish Nose Pickers
A dismissive nickname for the Scottish National Party among some grass-roots elements of other political parties in the North-east. The SNP appears not to feel terribly threatened by such biting satire.

Scour
Diarrhoea. Pronounced 'skoor'. North-east teachers have long since ceased being shocked by receiving parental sicknotes advising that 'Johnnie's got a terrible dose o the scour'. Mainly because it has taken several decades to get some parents to be sufficiently genteel to say scour. Also known, excuse me, as **the skitter** and **the rin-thins.**

Scran
Any reclaimed junk or under-the-counter handouts. 'Ye get some rare scran at car-boot sales.' 'Dinna buy envelopes; oor Gordon gets plenty scran fae his office.'

Scrape
A thin spread of butter or margarine. 'Are ye for some scrape on yer rowie, or jist a skite o jam?'

Scrat o a craiter
Literally, *a scratch of a creature. Someone of extremely diminished stature and girth.* 'Fit a scrat o a craiter. Ae puffa win' and she'll be awa.'

Scratcher
Bed. Derives from the days when farmworkers slept in straw-filled beds infested with corn lice and other such insects, leading to severely irritated skin and broken sleep. 'Weel, that's me awa tae ma scratcher.'

Screwed, punched or countersunk
Disorganised or, in other contexts, concussed. 'His boss dumped anither three wikks' paperwork on his desk and now he disna ken if he's screwed, punched or countersunk.'

Scud
Belt at school. Scud is the Aberdeen City word. The country word is **tawse**. 'I wis chaain in the class. The teacher gied me the scud/tawse.'

Scuddlers
Ragbag clothes. Any garments which are past their best and are fit only for the ragbag, or for gardening or DIY are said to be scuddlers. 'I'll awa and pit in anither twa-three dreel o tatties, my love.' 'As lang's ye've got on ye're scuddlers, please yersel.'

Seen til
Seen to. Said to anyone whose behaviour has been erratic and causing concern. 'You're needin seen til, you.'

Sees
May I have? 'Seesa shot o yer fitba.' 'Sees yer Beano ower here.'

Shady
Untrustworthy. 'Ye're nae giein a len o yer car tae Davie. He's shady.'

Sharger
A puny young animal; the runt of the litter. 'I dinna think that pup'll see oot the nicht. It's a sharger.' The word can also be a verb, meaning 'to ruin by indulgence'. 'Stop playin wi that kitten, lass, or ye'll sharger it.'

Sheen
Shoes. A single shoe is a **shee**. Two unmatched sheen are said to be **marless sheen** (*matchless shoes*).

Sheetin rubbits

Literally *shooting rabbits*, but used in farming communities to describe breaking violent wind. 'I widna aet ony mair o that lentil soup, Dosh, for ye'll be sheetin rubbits aa nicht.'

Shochle

Shuffle. Anyone who doesn't pick up their feet and walk smartly is said to shochle, but the crime is at its most serious on the dance-floor, where no one wants a shochler for a partner. 'For ony sake, Peter, is that you dancin or jist shochlin?'

Shoo

To sew. 'Mam, wid ye shoo on this shirt button for me?'

Shooderie

A man carrying any small child on his shoulders is giving the child a shooderie.

Shop-bocht

Ready-made. One of the greatest insults in the North-east house-wife's lexicon. 'Aathing on her table wis shop-bocht.' Any North-east homemaker is meant to have the skill, time and inclination to make jam, cakes, pies, soup and bread for herself, without relying on tins, jars or packets.

Shortsome

Anything which has passed the time agreeably has been shortsome. 'I didna mind ironin twenty-fower sarks. It wis shortsome.'

Shot

Drunk. 'We'd tae tak Wull hame in a cairtie. He wis fair shot.'

Showdies

Any arrangement which rocks back and forth. This can be at a funfair (showboats) or the gentle rocking of a mother trying to get her baby to sleep. 'I canna get young Aurora tae sleep ata, nae even wi showdies.'

Showies
Any small funfair which travels round rural towns, settling for two or three days at a time. 'Awa doon til the showies, Cheyenne, and see if ye canna win yersel a goldfish.'

Shrapnel
Small change. 'Gie's a tenner for this haunfae o shrapnel.'

Sikkin
Requiring. From the English 'seeking', this is standard Doric for any request. I've been in a Fraserburgh tearoom and had the waitress ask very courteously, 'And fit are ye sikkin?' I've also heard a very angry child throw a tantrum at being offered broccoli and bawl: 'I'm nae sikkin't.'

Singin
Excessively pungent. 'Awa and tak a sniff o Sandy ben in the public bar. His draaers are singin.' The implication is that the odour is so ripe that it can almost be heard.

Sit-in
Not an industrial protest, but a restaurant meal. Derives from the counter assistant at certain fish bars inquiring whether the patrons wish to consume the goods on the premises or to take them away to eat elsewhere, viz: 'Sit-in or tak-oot?'

Skinnymalink
A painfully thin person, hence the playground taunt: 'Skinnymalinky lang legs, wi umberella feet. Went til the picters and couldna get a seat.'

Skirlie
Favoured North-east delicacy made of oatmeal and onions, fried in

lard. Usually eaten with mashed tatties, green peas and a cup of milk. Sheer ambrosia, and totally calorie-free.

Skite
To slide. As opposed to 'be on the skite' which means to have an uproarious and alcoholic night out. 'Me and Joe's got affa sair heids the day. We wis oot on the skite till five.' It can also be a dash of liquid. 'Pit a skite o watter in ma dram, Tam.'

Skitter
An inconsequential amount, bordering on insult. 'Ye ca' that a denner for a workin man? Twa tatties and a skitter o mince?'

Skittery-dick
A prune. 'Ma man ate a hale tin o skittery-dicks. He wis up and doon aa nicht.' Not to be confused with **Peter Dick** (qv).

Sklyte
Onomatopoeic word meant to convey impact, usually of someone having an accident. 'She wis rinnin doon the hill, trippit and fell sklyte on her bum.'

Skoof
A swig. 'Are ye for a skoof o Lilt, Alice? It's diet.'

Skydiver
A particularly determined participant in the January sales. This has been coined by present-day shop-assistants in Aberdeen, who marvel at the mêlée when women spot bargains. It derives from the fact that, on spotting the bargain in a crowded store, the woman flings out both her arms and dives at the item as quickly as possible, lest someone else get there first. As a result, she looks uncannily as if she has just flung herself from a plane.

Skysie
Tight-fisted, mean. 'Can I hae a shot o yer car the nicht, dad? 'No.' 'Oh, dinna be skysie.'

Slappie
Nothing to do with physical abuse. A slappie (or a trackie) is *a narrow lane between buildings*. 'I wid hiv catched the blighter, bit he jinkit doon the slappie.'

Slater
Woodlouse. Or a roofing tradesman. The context usually makes it clear.

Sleekit
Sly or devious. Another marvellous Doric word which sounds exactly as its meaning suggests. 'There'll be tears afore lang wi that new wifie as club treasurer. There's something sleekit aboot her.'

Slider
Two scoops of ice-cream placed side by side and sandwiched between two wafers, one of which might be nougat-filled as a Sunday treat. 'I'll hae twa bugs o crisps, a bottle o ale, three tubes o Polos and a slider.'

Slivvers
Long dangles of saliva. 'Awa and dicht grannie's moo, Sylvia. She's terrible slivvery the day.'

Slivvers and snotters
An uncomplimentary description of a brood of children whose upbringing is judged to be less than satisfactory. 'He's nivver oot o the pub. She's nivver awa fae the bingo. Nae muckle winner the kids are aye slivvers and snotters.'

Slochin
Thirst-quenching. 'There's nithing mair slochin than a drink o Alford watter.' Except on the days it tastes like neat Domestos.

Slubbery
Anything excessively wet and warm. Onomatopoeic. Potatoes which have not been drained properly can be said to be slubbery. The

sensation of eating frogs' legs, I suppose, must be slubbery. But the word is used most often to describe excessively enthusiastic kissing. 'Thon wis an affa slubberin ye wis deein ahen the hall on Friday nicht.' 'I canna stand ma grannie's visits; she insists on giein me a slubbery kiss.'

Sma book
Really compact. An efficiently packed suitcase or a tightly packed parcel is said to be in 'sma book'.

Sma mooie
Small mouth. Said of any sulking child or woman. 'She's got a touch o the sma mooie.' Derives from that peculiar shrinkage of the lips whenever someone wishes silently to convey his extreme displeasure. Also referred to as **the lippie**, because the bottom lip trembles in fury or in barely controlled sobbing.

Smachrie
Sweets that are so cheap that handfuls can be bought for a few pennies. I've heard it applied to cheap jewellery, too, as an insult.

Smellies
Perfume. 'Ma man wis awa abroad on business. He stopped in by the Duty Free and bocht me some rare smellies.'

Smorin
Suffocating, but used most often of a bad head cold. 'Alison winna be at the school the day. She's smorin wi the caul.'

Sna mannie
Snowman. Subject of the Aberdeen playground rhyme, uttered always at the first fall of snow:

Sna mannie, sna mannie
Ding doon sna.
Ding doon a hunder
And I'll catch them aa.

Snuffie
A prostitute. 'Dinna you wander roon the herber at nicht, son. Ye'll be trippin ower snuffies.' This curious name is a fond tribute to an old Aberdeen character, Snuffie Ivy, whose reign as the city's principal lady of business was marked by her trademark drip at the end of her nose, causing her perpetually to sniff. So I'm told.

Something
A drink. 'Are ye for a something?' Also known as **a thochtie**.

Sookit
Adjective describing anything which looks drawn, crinkled or puckered. 'I've hid weet socks on a' day and ma feet's terrible sookit.' 'Elsie's lost twa steen in a fortnicht and she's lookin affa sookit aboot the face.' Also, any young man in the heat of a romantic clinch in a corner might be admonished with: 'Haud aff that kissin, Tam; ye'll hae her sookit dry.'

Soss
A minor mess. 'Gie the table a wipe, Mina. It's an affa soss o crumbs.'

Sotter
General disorder. 'Awa and tidy up yer bedroom, Jason. I've nivver seen sic a sotter.' One Monymusk person has tried to persuade me that several locals at Monymusk in the 1940s were exasperated by the poor sense of order of the prisoners in the POW camp which was situated in the area and decided to erect a warning sign. Helpfully, some of the village wags supposedly had a stab at translation, resulting in a sign reading: 'Sotters verboten.' Alas, the effort was largely wasted; most of the prisoners were Italian. A likely story.

Spad
A spade, but also to walk in a very clumsy, ungainly manner. 'Dod walks a'wye as if he wis spaddin up a neep park.' (George walks everywhere as if he were clumping through a field of turnips). It

derives from the farmer's and gardener's habit of measuring every-thing by spade lengths, when each stride approximates the length of a spade.

Spare
Unattached members of the opposite sex. 'Are ye gaun tae Shona's party? There'll be plenty o spare.'

Spaver
Trouser zip or buttons. A man of powerful libido is said to be 'louse wi the spaver' (loose with his trouser zip). Such a man might be advised to 'pit his brikks on back tae front'. A man appearing in public with his spaver accidentally open might be advised: 'Wullie, yer shoppie door's open' or 'Wullie, are ye sellin spunks (matches)?'

Speir the guts fae . . .
Ask repeatedly. There's no direct translation (nor does English offer a better alternative to this descriptive Doric phrase). Literally, to speir the guts fae is to ask questions repeatedly until the victim's stomach begins to ache. 'Dinna start newsin wi Dorothy, for she'll speir the guts fae ye.'

Spew
Vomit. 'Slow doon yer drivin, Arnold. I'm nae far aff spewin.' Comes from the Norwegian verb 'å spy ut', pronounced 'spee oot' (say it quickly). Note that in North-east Scotland you do not make someone spew, you 'gaur' them spew. 'If ye dinna pit that thing awa, Geordie, ye'll gaur me spew.' See also **tatties ower the side**.

Spew or a haircut
Describing any indecisive person. 'He disna ken if he wints a spew or a haircut.' There are other, less genteel, versions.

Spewin feathers
Exceptionally thirsty. 'What an affa day o heat. I'm spewin feathers.' One can also have **a moofae o dandruff**.

132

Spik o the place
Subject of community gossip. Anyone who has drawn attention to themselves through misdemeanour or glorious disregard for the prejudices and small-mindedness of others has become 'the spik o the place'. Used most notably of author James Leslie Mitchell who, as Lewis Grassic Gibbon, wrote most disparagingly of his home farming community, leading his family to say that he had made them 'the spik o the Mearns'. Also the title of a dictionary of modern North-east vernacular, I'm told.

Spikkin sweeties
Conversation lozenges, those small tablets of sugar which bore little mottos such as 'You're My Angel' and 'Say You're Mine'. 'Twinty Senior Service and a quarter o spikkin sweeties, please.' I've always thought there was an opening there for an enterprising North-east confectioner to come up with Doric conversation lozenges: 'Fit Like The Day?', 'Chaa Yer Lugs', 'Awa And Burst'.

Spit
Short for spitting image. 'She's jist her mither's spit.'

Spleet new
Factory-fresh. Used to differentiate between plain, common-or-garden new and absolutely brand spanking new, which is a pretty fine distinction. Said especially of cars. 'I see the Thomsons hiv anither spleet-new Mercedes. Far dis a bobby get that kinna money?' 'Overtime.'

Split The Win
Great Northern Road diverges on a very acute angle, becoming Causewayend and George Street. Split The Win is the name given to this junction, because it's so sharp that it's said to 'split the wind'.

Spud
Not a potato (that's a tattie). A spud is *a medium-to-large hole in a pair of stockings or tights*, seen to best effect on an amply upholstered

matron. 'That's an affa spud ye've got in yer stoackins the day, Ina.'
One needs only to see such a phenomenon to understand how the
name arose.

Spunks
Matches. One does not 'strike' a spunk. A spunk is 'crackit'. 'Oor
Wayne'll set the hoose on fire een o this days. He sits in his bedroom
crackin spunks.' A particularly angry glare is 'a look that wid crack
spunks'.

Spurtle
Carved and turned wooden stick for stirring porridge. Anyone who has
particularly thin and pale legs can be said to have **legs lik spurtles**.

Squeak
Any weekly paper. 'That wis a queer-like caption in the Inverurie
squeak.'

Stairvin
Freezing cold. Nothing to do with hunger. 'Shut that door and keep
the heat in; I'm stairvin ben here.'

Stammygaster
A profound shock. A marvellous Doric word which is still in regular
use. 'Ma brither's run aff wi the meenister. What a stammygaster!'

Stappit
Stuffed. 'We'll hae tae get the plumber oot. The drains are stappit.'
If anything is stuffed to bursting point, it is said to be **stappit fu**.
Many a Christmas lunch concludes with the entire assembly
confessing to being thus afflicted.

Steer
A seething crowd. 'Wisn't there an affa steer at Keith Show last wikk?'
Also, to stir, as in: 'Steer that porritch afore it sticks tae the boddim
o the pan.'

Steppies and stairies
A large brood of children; the time lapse between the production of each having been more or less equal. So called because a line-up for a family photograph shows the children at differing heights, according to their ages, and looking like a sequence of steps and stairs.

Stew
Dust. 'She ca's hersel a housewife, bit ony time I've been in her livinroom her sideboord's that covered in stew ye could draw picters.' Anyone who is particularly weak or ineffectual **couldna blaa the stew aff a bap.**

Stew and sma steens
Literally, *dust and small stones.* When someone makes a hasty exit, bystanders will observe wryly that 'ye couldna see him for stew and sma steens'.

Stew-collector
Table ornament. So called because it serves no useful purpose, but has to be dusted daily. 'Jeannie took me hame a china doll fae Butlin's. It's jist anither stew-collector.'

Stick bubbly
So there. 'My dad got a new car last wikk. It's a Fiat.' 'So? My dad got a new car last nicht, and it's a BMW. Stick bubbly.' Supposes that the person whose tale has been topped has burst into tears at being bettered (is bubbly).

Stick in!
Instruction to any child to make the most of the food just presented. In the recent past, this was also used to encourage any child to study hard at school. 'Stick in at yer lessons, Duncan.'

Sticky-willie
The tenacious weed which English people know as cleavers, and botanists as Galium aparine. Sticky-willies operate on a similar

principle to Velcro, in that minute hooks attach themselves to any passing animal or clothing. It is a thorough pest throughout the rural North-east. I've heard the term applied to anyone who is light-fingered or who is a known shoplifter, but not frequently. The usual term for that is **tarry-fingered** (pronounced without hard G).

Stinky Club
Any child who has done his best to avoid washing or any form of personal hygiene will be inspected disapprovingly by a parent, who will observe drily: 'Somebody's surely jined the Stinky Club.'

Stoonin
Throbbing. 'I've a stoonin heid wi ye playin yer drums.'

Stovie Dance
A pivot of the North-east social calendar. Whenever funds must be raised for a good cause in a parish, hamlet, village or small town, you may be sure that the means by which it will be achieved will be a Stovie Dance, whereby the evening's revelry will be punctuated at regular intervals by ample portions of stovies, cooked in the hall kitchen, whacked onto plates by brosey (qv) matrons and charged at exceptionally reasonable rates.

Stovies
Another North-east delicacy, originally sliced potatoes, onions, a knob of butter and finely chopped leftover beef, all slow-cooked together in a pan. Now made more commonly with minced beef. Always accompanied to best effect with an oatcake, some beetroot and a cup of milk.

Straaberry
Strawberry. The garden soft fruit, obviously, but also used to describe the nose of anyone whose drinking habits have blessed his nose with that peculiar purply-red hue and bulbous shape. 'Thon's an affa straaberry Dod's got nooadays.'

Stretchin

Embellishing a tale. 'Rab, I'm prepared tae believe ye saw Sophia Loren on yer hol'days in Rome, bit fin ye claim she invitit ye back til her hoose for a fly cup and a news, I doot ye're stretchin.' Another suitable word would be **slidin**. One could also be **comin the bug**.

Stunkit

Sulked. 'I dinna ken fit I said tae offend her, but Izzie's stunkit wi me.'

Sung

Singed. Said usually of burned food, and mostly of soup, especially soup that has been reheated too often. 'That micht hiv been a fine broth last wikk, Lottie, bit it's fairly sung noo.' Also: 'Can ee sing?' 'Ay, I've often sung the custard.'

Suppie

A very small amount. 'I canna hae ony o yer trifle, Mabel. I'm on a diet. Och, weel, maybe jist a suppie.'

Surely a lee

Must have been a lie. Retort to anyone who has forgotten what he was about to say. 'Ay, Charlie, that wis surely a lee.'

Sut

So. Used for emphasis in an argument. 'I will not.' 'Ye will sut.'

Sweelie

A small libation. 'Ye'll hae a dram, Charlie?' 'Na, I'd better awa hame.' 'Come awa, ye'll surely manage ae last drammie.' 'Och, a'richt, seein as it's yersel. Jist a sweelie.'

Sweetie-wife

Any effeminate man, but especially one older than 50. 'Alec's a bit o a sweetie-wife, bit he's hairmless.' Also known as a **jessie**.

Sweetie-wife

Sweir

To utter oaths. 'There's nae need tae sweir lik that, faither.' I was talking once to a Peterhead teacher of eight-year-olds who said she had asked her class what talents they thought their parents had. One boy asserted that his father 'wis a bliddy good sweirer'. Also . . .

Sweir

Reluctant. 'I wid fairly hae a go at sortin the mower masel, mither, bit I'm sweir in case I dinna dee't richt.'

Swick

To cheat or *a person who cheats.* 'I dinna play cards wi Ackie; nae since I fun oot that he swicks. His wife's a bit o a swick as weel.' One of the most biting satires seen on the North-east stage was one *Scotland the What?* character, invented by Steve Robertson and Buff Hardie. Cooncillor Alexander Swick was an Aberdeen bailie who was alive to every scam, fact-finding mission, expenses fiddle, free lunch, patronage and nepotism that he could sniff. Complete fiction, naturally.

Switch the station

No one changes channels on a TV in the North-east. We switch the station, turn ower, or gie't a twirl.

Syne

Ago. 'This is the same car I used lang syne.' It can also mean *then*. 'Syne she drappit doon deid, jist lik that. Nae even a cheerio.'

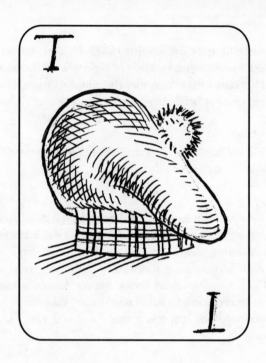

T

Tabbie
Cigarette dog-end. 'Abbie's fairly hit a roch patch. Ye see him doon at the herber pickin tabbies aff the pavement.'

Tak a tellin
Heed a warning. 'She widna tak a tellin, and now she's mairriet him.'

Tak a tummle
To trip and fall. Alternatively, to take stock of one's personal circumstances. 'Josie took a tummle and skinned her knees.' 'Dougie wis nivver oot o trouble wi the bobbies, bit he took a tummle til himsel and now he's learnin tae be a meenister.'

Tak aa
School-attendance inspector. Truancy officer. Official sent to investigate why a child has not been attending school. 'I've nivver been sae black affrontit. Fa cam til the door this mornin? The tak aa, that's fa.'

Tak ee or takee
The North-east version of the playground chasing game, tag.

Tak ma haun
An offer of support, as in: 'Tak ma haun, ma trusty freen', but more usually a warning to a child of impending physical punishment. 'Fiona, if you dinna stop bouncin on the settee wi yer fool feet, I'll tak ma haun aff the side o yer heid.'

Tak the len
Take advantage of. 'Annie's a gweed-hertit sowel, bit that femly o hers jist taks the len o her.'

Tally
Any Italian-owned café. 'Ye'll nivver beat a Tally for an ice-cream.' Those towns fortunate enough to have had two such establishments (such as Grantown-on-Spey) usually differentiated between the two by labelling them the Top Tally and the Bottom Tally, depending on their location on the main street. The viscous raspberry sauce squirted on cappies and sundaes was sometimes known as **Tally's bleed**.

Tap line
Pre-tax earnings. 'Fit's yer tap line this wikk, Pat?' Derives from the figure's position on the payslip. The tap line is also the most important point on the agenda for any meeting.

Tap o da's egg
The very best. 'Ma quinie means aathing tae me. She's jist the tap o da's egg.'

Target

A sartorial disaster. See also **Ticket**. 'I widna buy that frock if I wis you, Janet. Ye look a richt target.'

Taste

To taint something. 'Keep the soap pooder awa fae the loaf, or it'll taste it.' One could equally use the verb **smell**.

Tattie-masher

Prize marble. 'That's some tattie-masher ye've got there, Doddie.' A tattie-masher is also the kitchen implement for turning boiled potatoes into mashed potatoes.

Tatties

Potatoes, obviously, but also an Aberdonian expression meaning 'finished'. 'Heather, if ye dinna get that mess cleaned up afore the boss comes back ye'll be tatties.' Short for **Tatties ower the side**, an expression from trawling's heyday. I've found two possible derivations for this. One group holds that it describes the act of throwing any surplus scraps of unusable grub overboard at the end of the meal. The other group asserts that it refers to seasickness, when the victim's recent meal (the tatties) would be vomited into the ocean (ower the side). In any case, the meaning of both is the same – finished.

The Tatties

Potato-harvesting. Before the advance of farm mechanisation, schoolchildren throughout the North-east would be dispatched during the October school holidays round a sequence of neighbourhood farms to gather potatoes. The October school holidays are still referred to as the Tattie Holidays, even although almost no schoolchildren undertake the task.

Tee til

Next to, against. 'Jist you tak yer voluptuous self ower here darlin, and sit yersel tee til me.'

142

Teenie fae Troon
Any woman who fancies herself as someone of style or social position.
'Tak a look at Teenie fae Troon. She thinks she's something.'

Teet-bo
Very difficult to translate, but this is what a North-east adult says in a high-pitched, comic voice to a very small child when peeping out repeatedly from behind a cushion, for example, and pretending to surprise the infant. The closest English word, I suppose, is peeka-boo. Teet-bo usually occasions much gurgling and giggling on the part of the child but, if the adult is in the slightest facially challenged, can lead equally to protracted and piercing howls.

Teeth lik a set o burglar's tools
Uneven in oral structure. 'I've seen some pianna keys in ma time, but the new barman's got teeth lik a set o burglar's tools.'

Tekkie
A very brief visit. 'I'll jist tak a tekkie in by the bookies.'

Ten-to-two
Splay-footed. 'Oor Erchie wis put oot o the Army for his ten-to-two feet.' Derives from the position of hands on a clockface.

Teuchter
Son or daughter of the rural North-east. See also **Toonser**.

That'll see me oot
That will be the last one I buy before I die. Said jocularly by any older person purchasing a new car or a new suit. If such a person were asked how he was feeling, he might say: 'Anither clean sark and that'll be me.'

Thin as a skinned rubbit
And that's pretty thin. One can also be **a rickle o beens** (a pile of bones) or **as thin as the links o the crook** (as thin as the leg of a shepherd's staff).

Teuchter

144

Thon wye
Effeminate, of a homosexual bent. 'I feel hert sorry for Rosie. What a work she put intil that loon, and now here's him knittin his ain cardigans and bakin fairy cakes. I aye thocht he wis a bittie thon wye.' Such a chap might also be said to be **a bittie Mamsy** (a mother's boy).

Thoomed piece
A sandwich in which the butter has been spread on by the thumb, rather than with a knife.

Throwe haun
I'm stumped for even a vague translation of this. Literally, it means *through hand*, but the context is a conversation in which matters, acquaintances and community news is raked over and sorted out. This is 'takkin things/freens/the news throwe haun'.

Through the bree
Of low intelligence. 'I dinna ken fit wye they've taen him on as an apprentice. His heid wis through the bree lang ago.' Derives from boiling potatoes for so long that they turn into mush. The tatties and the liquid become inseparable, thus the tatties are through the bree.

Ticht
Suffering a shortage. 'Ma mither wid mak mair hame-made wine, bit she's affa ticht for corks.'

Ticket
One who is dressed badly. 'I dinna ken fit Annie's thinkin aboot, pittin her faimly oot dressed lik thon. Ye see some affa tickets nooadays.' See also **Target**.

Timmer up
To sort out or to chastise. 'I made a surprise visit tae the buildin-site and the labourers wis aa sittin on their backsides drinkin Dazzle. I timmered them up in twa minutes flat.'

Tinkie

Any travelling person. There was no criticism or condescension in the word. It was simply a statement of fact. That is not the case with tink, a highly emotive way to describe a quarrelsome or sluttish woman. 'Yer mither's jist a tink' has upset many a North-east schoolchild and has helped spark a few court cases.

Tinkie's tae

Modern method of making tea, by dipping a teabag into a mug of boiling water. To anyone over 50, this is a sign of lax housekeeping and poor kitchen standards. Young people hoping to impress future in-laws with their domestic skills are advised to get out the teapot.

Tinkie's tartan

The pattern of blue veins and red blotches seen most commonly on the legs of elderly women, or on those who have fallen asleep in front of a fire.

Toad-in-the-hole

The sausage-and-egg dish which remains the saddest episode in school meals in the North-east. It had to be removed wholesale from the prescribed menus in the late 1960s when pupils throughout Aberdeenshire refused en masse to eat it. One wag observed: 'They should hiv taen it oot o the hole.'

Toffee

Sweetmeat made by simmering condensed milk, butter and sugar. Elsewhere in Scotland, this is known as tablet. In the North-east, it's Swiss Milk Toffee, a staple of every WRI sale of work since time began. The mixture is poured into large, flat, oblong trays and allowed to cool. Then it's cut into large squares and wrapped in greaseproof paper, usually with '60p' written somewhere in Biro. Toffee quality is judged by how well the sugar has dissolved. Bad toffee is hard and grainy. Good toffee begins melting the moment it hits the tongue and has no hint of sugar crystals at all. I'm told the secret is in cooking as slowly as possible, with constant stirring.

Expert toffee-makers, consequently, can be identified by muscles that would win prizes in bodybuilding competitions. By the way, the brown chewy lumps that elsewhere are known as toffees are known in the North-east as caramels.

Tongue that wid clip cloots
Speech so abrasive that it would leave cloth in tatters. Doesn't translate well, but used to describe that breed of woman who takes no prisoners and is not shy of letting fly with ripe language in defence of that which she holds dear. 'I widna cross her if I wis you. She's got a tongue that wid clip cloots.'

Took the gate
Ran off at high speed. 'I telt him I micht be pregnant and he took the gate.'

The Toon
Aberdeen. No person from the rural North-east goes to Aberdeen. They ging tae The Toon.

Toonser
An Aberdonian. An uncomplimentary description of a son or daughter of the Granite City, used exclusively by those born and bred in the country. 'She's fairly got airs and graces, bit she's jist a Toonser.' Correspondingly, an Aberdonian will refer equally disparagingly to country-dwellers as **Teuchters**.

Tooshtie
An extremely small amount, barely perceptible. 'I'm on a diet. Nae mair than a tooshtie butter on ma toast, if ye please.' Not to be confused with . . .

Toosties
Wire hair-curlers. 'Flora winna be minutes. She's takkin oot her toosties.'

Top show
Exceptionally good. More of a young North-easter's expression than a traditional one. 'I saw ye left the club early last nicht wi thon hunky young gym teacher, Felicity. Wis everything as ye expectit?' 'Oh, top show, Angela. Absolutely top show.'

Torn-faced
Description of anyone who looks miserable.

Tractor ile
Tea or coffee that is far too strong. 'Mercy, Betty, that's tractor ile ye're giein me the day.' Strong tea is also said to be **stewed**.

Trades
The July fortnight's holiday in Aberdeen, in which manual workers and factory workers head for sunnier climes. 'I canna get a plumber for love nor money.' 'That's because it's Trades.'

Trock
Rubbish. 'The sign says Antiques Shop, bit there's only aul trock inside.'

Tummle the cat
Child's somersault. 'The bairn's as happy as onything; oot on the back green tummlin the cat.'

Turra
Aberdeenshire agricultural town of Turriff. Famous once for the Turra Coo and now for the Turriff Show, one of the few remaining agricultural shows in the North-east calendar and a magnet which draws entries and visitors from throughout Scotland every August. The event is frequently shortened to just 'Turra'. 'An affa number o entries at Turra this 'ear.' Like its nearest rival, Keith Show, its success is out of all proportion to the size of its home town. It's probably a misapprehension, but it always seems to be raining at

Turriff Show, which led to the joke of two North-east men wandering, lost, in the Sahara. They stop in the blaze of 140° F heat and one turns to the other. 'Fit day is't the day?' 'Aagust the Sivventh.' The first man peers up at unrelenting sunshine and says: 'Man, they're gettin a gran day for Turra.'

Twa bob in the poun
Devoid of commonsense. 'I widna bother gettin involved wi Charlie's sister. She's twa bob in the poun, thon craiter.' Such a person could also be **short o a shillin.**

Twa bubbles aff the centre
Used to describe someone who is eccentric or bordering on stupid. Comes from the building trade, and the use of a spirit level. 'Did ye see that reader's letter in the daily paper the day? Fa ivver wrote thon's definitely twa bubbles aff the centre.'

Twa faul
Bent double or, more literally, *folded in two.* Can be used of paper or cardboard, but more often used of an elderly person with a pronounced stoop. 'What a peer craiter Mrs Duncan's turned. I saw her gaun her messages last nicht and she's nae far aff twa faul.'

Tyauve
A struggle. Pronounced 'chaav' and sometimes spelled that way. Used to best effect in that old North-east cry of weariness at the end of a hard working day: 'It's a sair tyauve for a half-loaf.' Also a standard riposte to an inquiry after one's health, viz: 'Fit like the day?' 'Tyauvin.'

U

Up in a lowe

Consumed by flames. 'Did ye nae hear the sireen? Did ye nae see aa the blue lichts? Norman's shed gaed up in a lowe last nicht. Nae even a spad left.' An especially voracious fire is said to be **a blue lowe**.

Up the golden staircase

Dead. 'Peer Annie. That's her up the golden staircase. Still, she's better aff awa.'

Up the wrang close

Up the wrong lane. Doric's version of 'You're barking up the wrong

Up the golden staircase

tree.' 'Ye'll nivver guess fit she's deen noo.' 'Crashed her car?' 'No, ye're up the wrang close there.'

Up the wrang dreel
Up the wrong row in the garden/field. Rural equivalent of **up the wrang close**.

V

Varsity

University of Aberdeen. No genuine North-east person refers to this great educational institution as the Uni, as other parts of Scotland refer to their universities. It's always 'the varsity', as in: 'Frances is at the varsity studying criminal psychology and industrial pyrotechnology – fibs and squibs'. In the use of 'varsity', we are in the good company of such as Oxford and Cambridge. However, since Aberdeen once had two universities when the whole of England could only rustle up a couple, perhaps we should say that Oxford and Cambridge are in the good company of Aberdeen.

Waak up and doon
Futile advice to a fractious child who is profoundly bored. 'Awa and waak up and doon a while.' A crueller version would be 'Awa oot and play on the dual-carriageway.'

Wackit
Mis-shapen. Said mostly of clothes which have not stood up to washing and have shrunk, discoloured or otherwise warped. 'That's ma Sunday cardigan come oot o the machine wackit.'

Walker's Bus
The North-east version of Shanks' Pony. 'No, ye canna see me hame

fae the dance. I'd raither tak Walker's Bus.' The phrase **Shanks' meer**
(*Shanks' mare*) is also used.

Waste o time gaun hame
Said of any frail person at a funeral.

Watter made waur
Weak tea. Said by someone who would have preferred a plain drink
of water than to have it ruined by a quick dip of a teabag and then
passed off as a genuinely satisfying cuppie. 'Forty pee for thon? It
wis nithing bit watter made waur.'

Watterie
The loo. 'Ma mither canna come til the door. She's in the watterie
readin the People's Freen.' Some people use the word **Sitooterie**, *the*
place where one sits out, although there are dangers here now that
Sitooterie can also mean *a consevatory.* The potential of such confusion hardly bears thinking about. People who are dismissive of the
current fashion for conservatories describe them, disparagingly, as
lean-tees (*lean-tos*), because they sit uneasily with the design of the
host house and look supposedly like nothing more than lean-to
sheds.

Weel-fired
Baked for slightly longer than its allotted time. Anything in the
baker's window which is slightly darker than usual can be said to be
'weel-fired'. 'Granda likes a weel-fired buttery.' However, in the
domestic context, 'weel-fired' is usually just a synonym for charcoal,
despite the fervent denials of the home-baker. 'Ma rock cakes are
nae brunt. They're jist weel-fired.'

Weel on
Drunk. 'Dinna gie Sandy anither dram, barman. He's weel on as it
is.'

Weel on

Weersis
Our or *ours*. North-east child's attempt at the English plural posses-
sive. I used to think this was a simple misunderstanding by one or
two children, but I've since heard it so frequently and in so many
villages that it must have become part of the idiom or dialect.
'Come and see weersis new car.'

Weldies
Wellington boots. 'Pit on yer weldies and come and help in the
gairden.'

Went
Aberdeen City's past participle of the English verb 'to go'. 'Far's
Julian?' 'He's went hame.' In the rural hinterland, the equivalent
word is 'gaen'.

The wheels fell aff
Idiomatic expression to bring down to earth someone who brags
about possessions or who has ideas above his station. 'I've got a
lovely Indian writing-desk from the pre-Raj period in ebonised
amboyna. Found it at a little antique shop in the Old Town. It was
a snip. The owner clearly didn't know what a treasure he had. I felt
almost guilty at the pittance I paid for such a lovely piece.' 'Aye, we'd
een o them bit the wheels fell aff.'

Wheepit
Whipped. Could be used of cream, I suppose, but more often used
to express speed. 'The car wheepit through the village at an affa
lick.' 'She'd wheepit the sark aff him afore he'd time tae say No.'

Whoop-de-do
Supposed expression of delight, but dripping with sarcasm. 'I see we're
gettin anither ten-poun Christmas bonus this 'ear. Whoop-de-do.'

Widdie
A small wood, but also a generic term for any cheap cigarette. Derived

from that old favourite, the Woodbine. 'Ony Widdies on ye, Tam? I'm gaspin.'

Widna bother ma erse
I have no intention of troubling myself.

Wiggy Jim
Any judicial person wearing a wig, but most often used of the sheriff at a sheriff court. 'The Wiggy Jim said he wis awardin ma wife fifty poun because she'd putten up wi ma bad behaviour for sae lang. I said I wid see if I could chip in a coupla quid masel.'

Winnie
Good fortune. A North-east person does not win a raffle, does not win at the bingo, and does not win the Lottery. He 'has a winnie'.

Wint
A lacking in the IQ department, being worryingly eccentric or simply vacant. 'Hiv ye seen the new boy in the General Office? There's a wint thonder.'

Wirds are win'
Words are wind. Of all the phrases which came my way during the researches for *Spik o the Place*, this was the one which summed up North-east philosophy most neatly. Words are worthless, it's actions that count. 'Tony Blair? A moofae o teeth spewin fine wirds, bit wirds are win'.' A similar homily would be **Fair wirds winna bile the pot** (*fair words won't cook anything*).

Wired up wrang
Describing anyone whose behaviour is aggressive or plain stupid. 'A walk doon Union Street on a Friday nicht shows ye that young fowk nooadays are jist wired up wrang.'

Wise up
Come to your senses. An expression used chiefly by younger people in

which they profess their disbelief at another's behaviour or assertions. 'Ye woke up in the middle o the nicht and Mel Gibson wis in yer bedroom? Wise up, Fiona.'

Woolmanhill
An area of Central Aberdeen razed for the construction of a large round-about. It was notable for being the site of the casualty hospital serving the whole of Aberdeen, and had been a medical site for at least three centuries. Some older Aberdonians still announce that they are 'awa tae Woolmanhill' to have a sudden wound treated, even although the Accident and Emergency Department moved a couple of miles west to Foresterhill 20 years ago.

Wrang spy
Wrong guess. An Aberdeen expression said to any child who has picked hastily or answered wrongly. 'Fitna haun's the sweetie in?' 'That een.' 'No, nithing there. Wrang spy.'

Y

Yackered
Exhausted. A marginally more genteel form of 'knackered'.

Ye widna need tae be
You wouldn't need to be. Many sentences begin with these words, implying frustration or resignation. For instance, if two people have waited for half an hour for a bus service which is supposed to run every ten minutes, they might say: 'Ye widna need tae be in a hurry.' If someone has just seen a belligerent drunk ushered from his company, he might observe philosophically: 'Ye widna need tae be easy offendit.' And so on.

Ye'll catch flees
A gentle suggestion to anyone who is wandering around with his mouth open, the implication being that, unless he shuts it, he will swallow insects.

Ye'll ken me next time
Statement delivered vigorously by someone who feels that a passer-by has been staring at him. In similar circumstances, anyone who asks: 'And fit are ee starin at?' might be treated to the reply, 'Lord knows; the ticket's faan aff.'

Ye're at yer untie's
Literally, *you're at your aunt's house.* This idiom is still in frequent use whenever a child is urged to help himself to food on the table while visiting someone else's home, whether or not the hostess is an aunt. 'Come on noo, young Simon, aet up; ye're at yer untie's.' The extended version implies that the hostess cannot see what is being eaten, so it wouldn't matter in any case how much the child consumed: 'Ye're at yer untie's and she's blin.'

Yestreen
Yesterday or *last night.* The exact meaning depends on the age of the person using the word. An elderly North-easter will use yestreen to mean 'at any point yesterday'. A middle-aged one will mean 'last night, from about 6 p.m. or later'. 'Did ye ging oot tae the pub yestreen?' 'Wis thon nae an affa day o win' yestreen?' Often, the Y is not pronounced.

Yokie
Feeling itchy. 'I've affa yokie feet.' Also, a peculiar form of cruelty perpetrated among schoolboys. The assailant rushes up behind the victim, clutches the victim's hips, thereby locating the sides of the victim's underpants. Still gripping the underpants, the assailant tugs sharply upwards, compressing the victim's reproductive accoutrements with such speed and pressure that the pain is truly

Ye'll ken me next time

163

excruciating. The victim, now with tears in his eyes and his stomach in his throat, has just been treated to 'a yokie'.

Yum-yum
A sickly confection of sweet dough, roughly 6 inches x 2 inches x 1 inch, twisted through 90 degrees halfway along and smothered in watery icing. It's a relative newcomer on the North-east patisserie scene and, in my book, you're better off with a Kit-Kat.

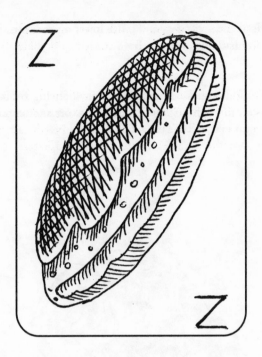

Z

Zatny affa?

Isn't that terrible? Expression used by anyone seeking conversational agreement about how despicable something is. 'The bank charged forty poun tae close ma deid uncle's accoont. Zatny affa?' The standard reply is: "At's affa, 'at.'

Zinc eyntment

Zinc ointment. Nothing to do with pharmaceuticals. This is the nasty, cloying, synthetic cream which bakers used in flans and cream cakes because genuine dairy cream would have gone off too quickly. The use of the phrase has been extended to cover any food which feels artificial and second-rate. 'I'll hae fower o yer éclairs, baker, as lang's they're nae zinc eyntment.'

Zube

A fool. A middle-aged person's expression, deriving from the old cough sweet, for anyone who is devoid of commonsense. 'Dinna believe fit Jim telt ye. Jim's jist a Zube.'

Zinc eyntment

Homilies

Aa yer taste's in yer moo.
All your taste is in your mouth. Often heard at dances in the 1940s, 1950s and 1960s, usually after a spat between two women. One resorts to an outburst which she imagines will crush the other, and usually the Achilles heel is deemed to be her dress sense. 'Ye think that's you dolled-up? Aa yer taste's in yer moo, lassie.'

As muckle eese as a left-handit hen.
Which isn't particularly useful, obviously. Also, **as muckle eese as Vaseline for a timmer leg.**

Aul age disna come itsel.
Growing old doesn't just involve the passing of time. Assorted aches, pains and ailments are inevitable, too.

Belly keeps the back up.
Full strength and vigour come from a hearty diet. 'Aet up, Tam. Ye've a full day's wark in front o ye, and it's the belly keeps the back up.'

Blaa the spokes fae the postie's bike.
Describing an exceptional gale. 'What an affa day o' win. It wid blaa the spokes fae the postie's bike.'

A blin mannie on a bike widna see it.
A blind man on a bike wouldn't see it. Used to reassure someone that an imperfection is so small that no one will notice. Conversely, this can equally be a dry dismissal of the very notion that something is almost invisible. 'Dinna worry, Mirabelle. I dinna think onybody'll see that lovebite.' 'Hmph. A blin mannie on a bike widna see it.'

Born the year o the short crap.
Anyone who is of short stature is said to be 'born the year o the short crap'. Note that 'crap' in Doric means 'crop', as in agriculture.

Canna sell the coo and sup the milk.
You can't have it both ways.

Chaa nails and spit roost.
Said of any well-built man who knows how to take care of himself. 'Dinna cross the foreman. He chaas nails and spits roost.'

Couldna tackle a plate o broth!
Shouted at any unfortunate footballer deemed to be slacking. Any food may be inserted here, but the sentiment is identical.

Crack in the lug wi a weet dishcloot.
It might be said of any sudden misfortune that 'at least it's better than a crack in the lug wi a weet dishcloot.' The English equivalent, I suppose, is 'a slap in the face with a wet haddock'.

Dinna gut till ye get.
Doric's version of 'Don't count your chickens until they're hatched'. The Doric version takes fishing as its motif, implying that you can't gut fish that you don't have.

Doon the Dee on a digestive.
Aberdeen's equivalent of Glasgow's 'up the Clyde on a banana'. A reminder to anyone that you are not as green as you are cabbage-looking. 'Hey, min. D'ye think I cam doon the Dee on a digestive?' Also: 'Doon the Dee on a banana-boat.'

Eneuch tae gaur yer lugs bleed.
Used to describe any garrulous or talkative person. 'Tom came back fae his holiday in New York last wikk. Fit wi the photies and that, it wis eneuch tae gaur yer lugs bleed.'

Fa cowpit your cairtie?
Who rattled your cage? Who upset you?

Feart for the death ye'll nivver dee.
An instruction to any timorous or nervous person not to be so frightened for herself. 'Dinna worry aboot fleein tae London, Nellie. Ye're feart for the death ye'll nivver dee.'

Fine boy fin he's sleepin.
Said of any tiresome individual, the implication being that he's a thorough pest in every waking moment.

Fit div feel loons ken?
A dry response to having a mistake pointed out. 'So Geneva's nae the capital o Switzerland? Ach weel; fit div feel loons ken?'

Fit's afore ye winna ging by ye.
Pure fatalism. There's no point in worrying about the future because it will happen, anyway.

Flee low, flee lang.
Keep your head down.

Folly me and yer tackets'll nivver roost.
Follow me and your boot studs will never rust. Loses a lot in the translation into English, as you can tell. An exhortation to join a winning team; the implication being that hard work and effort will be rewarded.

Gie a beggar a bed and he'll pey ye wi a louse.
One good turn deserves another, but very rarely gets it.

Gweed gear comes in sma book.
Good things come in small parcels. Usually uttered by the North-east's shortest citizens, it must be said.

Haud up yer heid lik a thristle.
Be a proud Scot.

Hips and haas, frosts and snaas.
A profusion of rosehips forewarns of a hard winter. One of many meteorological sayings in the North-east.

His wheel's turnin, bit his hamster's deid.
Used to describe anyone of slow wit. Similar to 'twa sandwiches short o a picnic'.

Hisna the strength o a sookin teuchit.
Hasn't the strength of a sucking lapwing. Describes anyone who looks weak. By the way, the **teuchit storm** is rough weather in March, named because the teuchits are arriving in the North-east to begin nesting.

Hiv ye been ootside the Tivoli?
Said to anyone who has a large handful of small change. The implication is that the person has been busking to the queues outside the old Tivoli Theatre in Guild Street, Aberdeen. Despite the fact that the Tivoli's variety-show days ceased in the 1960s, this phrase is still used frequently in Aberdeen.

I could sook the face aff her.
One young man's confession to his friend that he lusts for a particular young woman.

I hinna seen that since . . .
   Cripple Annie swum the Channel
   God wis last at Fordyce
   the days o paraffin phones
   the days o timmer bilers.

If that's wir tea we've hid it.
Meaningless phrase used as a joke about a rather slim meal. One might also say: 'That'll dee me till I hae something tae eat.'

It aa gings doon the same road.
Said to anyone who fusses excessively over food. 'Nivver mind stuffin the mushrooms, Ina; it aa gings doon the same road.'

I've gien awa bigger tips.
Jocular dismissal of someone's wonder at a mention of a large amount of money, or bragging about an excessive salary or a big gambling win.

Kittle tae wakken sleepin doggies.
Tickle to waken sleeping dogs. In other words, start very tentatively before you make sweeping changes.

Lean on yer ain denner.
Heard frequently in queues at bus-stops and taxi-ranks after an evening's alcoholic entertainment. One party, on the point of exhaustion, slumps against a companion. The companion finds the weight too much to bear and instructs the slumpee to stand up for himself. 'Wull, wid ye lean on yer ain denner?'

Like a sheep lookin throwe blin drift.
Like a sheep looking through a blizzard. Said of anyone whose haircut is shaggier or fringe longer than it might be. 'She thinks she looks like a model, but she's mair o a sheep lookin throwe blin drift.'

Loudest bummer's nae aye the best bee.
A variation of 'Empty barrels make the most noise'. In a similar vein, **Shalla watters mak the maist din** and **The bonnie birdie's aye the warst singer**.

Mair degrees than a thermometer.
Exceptionally gifted in the grey-matter department. 'Young Wullie next door? What a clivver loon. He's got mair degrees than a thermometer.'

A moo lik a breid draaer.
A mouth like bread drawer. Bread was kept not in a breadbin but in the widest drawer of a chiffonier. Hence: 'See that Carol Smillie, she's got a moo lik a breid draaer. And that Cherie Blair's the same.' Also: 'The last time I saw a moo like that, there wis a hook in it.'

Nae a bed made, nor a po teemed.
Not a bed made, nor a chamberpot emptied. Once the mid-morning cry of all harassed housewives. 'Look at the time! Ten o'clock and nae a bed made, nor a po teemed!' Now heard increasingly from stressed staff in offices and workplaces throughout the North-east as companies expect ever more effort from a dwindling number of employees.

Nae a bonnie loon, bit a fine loon.
Description of someone who is not particularly handsome, but whose inner personal qualities more than make up for that lack.

Nae even time tae tak aff her sark.
Anything which happens suddenly can be said to have happened so quickly that one had 'nae even time tae tak aff her sark'.

Nae worth a tinkie's fart.
Which isn't worth much, as you would understand.

Needless poorin watter on a drooned moose.
It's pointless to pour water on a drowned mouse. Don't throw good money after bad, in other words.

Nithing in his heid bit fit the speen pits in.
Nothing in his head except whatever the spoon puts in. Said of anyone who is particularly empty-headed or foolish.

Nivver dirt on yer ain doorstep.
Don't cause yourself problems in your own neck of the woods.

Pairt sma tae ser' aa.

When visitors arrive unexpectedly at mealtimes (which happens a lot in the North-east), the host or hostess brings in extra supplies or, more usually, simply ekes out what exists already into smaller portions, hence: *By dividing smaller, we can serve everyone.* English hasn't the same ring.

Pit canna in yer pooch and try again.

Don't give up. This is Doric's encouragement to tenacity. Few people are despised as much in the North-east as those who give up at the first hurdle. On wailing that: 'I canna dee't', they are told swiftly to 'Pit canna in yer pooch and try again.'

Proodest nettle grows in a midden.

The tallest nettle grows in a dunghill. In other words, the flashiest person is usually mired in trouble.

Roon yer hert lik a hairy worm.

What any thick, warming comfort food will do on a cold winter's night: 'Here's a bowlie o fine thick tattie soup tae ye. That'll ging roon yer hert lik a hairy worm.' Older readers might say **Roon yer hert lik new flannin**, flannin being the thick flannel undervest bought new once a year.

Saves spilin anither couple.

Said on observing a husband-wife or boyfriend-girlfriend combination in which neither party is likely to feature on a magazine cover or win a Mr or Miss Personality competition. The derivation is simple: by pairing deeply unappealing people with each other, reasonably attractive souls are free to find others of like mind or appearance. 'That new couple next door hiv baith got faces lik saft tatties.' 'Ach, weel, it saves spilin anither couple.'

Say fit ye like, hear fit ye dinna like.

The North-east's version of 'Judge not lest ye be judged.' Given the currency of gossip, plenty of people should heed this.

Seen wiser aetin girss.
I've seen wiser eating grass. Said of anyone whose IQ is thought to be inferior to that of a cow or a sheep.

She let aa the bunnets ging by, wytin for a lum hat.
She let all the ordinary beaux pass her by, waiting for a real catch. Said of any elderly spinster deemed to have been too choosy among boyfriends in her young day. Conversely, in her defence: 'Mugs is aye taen first. The best china's left on the shelf.'

Shitey cloot.
A soiled rag. The phrase is used most notably in the Aberdeen rhyme which is directed at anyone who seems to be dejected or in low spirits. 'Norman, Norman, there's nae doot. Ye're stannin there lik a shitey cloot.'

Somebody's surely come by the smiddy.
Sarcastic response by the victim of an unwelcome joke, the idea being that the joker has evidently had his wits sharpened by the blacksmith.

Starts lik a threid and ends lik cairt raip.
It starts like a thread and ends like cart rope. Mountains soon grow out of molehills. A jibe at the North-east's fondness for gossip and for building a tale until it bears little resemblance to what actually happened. Each village or town appears to have its own version. At Keith, they say, 'If ye trip in Mid Street, ye've broken yer leg afore ye land.' At Rhynie, it's 'If ye fart at the tap eyn o Rhynie, it's intil a hillock a dirt by the time it's oot at the fit.' You get the idea.

Them that his aye gets.
Good fortune smiles on those who are already fortunate. 'Elsie won at the bingo last wikk, she'd fifty poun aff the Premium Bonds and now here's her a Lottery millionaire. Them that his aye gets.' Older

people in Aberdeen itself might describe Elsie as 'a gaun that's aye gettin'.

There's aye a something.
Probably the single saying which captures the ethos of wry, dry, stoicism in adversity of the North-east better than any other. Made famous in 1933 by Doric poet Dr Charles Murray, who titled a poem thus. I can illustrate best by having you imagine two North-east men leaning at the bar having a private discussion when one says: 'I'm at the end o ma rope, Wullie. Last nicht, the dog wis flattened wi a bus; the kids are up in coort the morn for stealin; the wife's run aff wi her boss; ma mither's crashed her car; ma faither's been telt he's got a wikk tae live if he's lucky, and ma business his gaen doon the tubes, so that's me bankrupt and nae a penny tae ma name.' 'Losh, there's aye a something.'

Tichter than a dyeuck's chairlie.
Tighter than a duck's behind. Exceptionally parsimonious. A dyeuck's chairlie is thought to be the tightest thing known to science because of its ability to keep out water, hence: 'Eb's tichter than a dyeuck's chairlie – and that's watterticht.'

Washin like the bells that nivver rang.
Any washing which is hung out to dry and is caught in a rainstorm hangs heavy and soaking on the line.

Watter far the stirkie droons.
There's water where the cattle drown. The North-east's version of 'no smoke without fire', used by hopelessly sanctimonious people, I've always thought.

We aa come tae ae door at nicht.
We all arrive at one door at night. Meaning that death is the same for rich or poor, lowly or exalted.

Weet feet and dreepin nibs.
Wet feet and running noses. Warning of a rainy day. 'Nae picnic the day, kids. It wid be weet feet and dreepin nibs.'

Wid ye like a speen?
Would you like a spoon? Said to anyone who is trying to cause trouble or dissent. The implication is that if the person had a spoon, he would make a much better job of stirring up trouble.

Winna get muckle change oot o . . .
Won't get much change out of . . . Idiomatic, so this doesn't translate easily. Used to describe a profoundly dour or taciturn person, usually a man. 'There's nae pint tryin tae hae a news wi Arthur. Ye winna get muckle change oot o Arthur. Naebody gets muckle change oot o Arthur.'

Ye canna mak honey oot o hens' dirt.
The North-east's version of 'you can't make a silk purse out of a sow's ear.'

Yer dowp's lik a face tae them.
Your behind's like a face to them. When any older North-east woman has to make a rare trip to hospital for an intimate examination, and is aghast at the prospect of undressing in front of medical professionals, a true friend will remind her that the medical professionals will be unfazed by the experience because they see such sights every working day. Indeed, so familiar are those sights that they have become just as familiar as faces. 'Dinna worry aboot yer MoT, Ina. Yer dowp's jist lik a face tae them.'

Ye're a better door than a windae.
Said by someone whose view of something has been blocked (TV, for instance, or a Royal walkabout) to the person whose ample form is doing the blocking. 'Excuse me, Mr Pavarotti, bit ye're a better door than a windae.'

Ye've a neck for aathing bit soap and watter.
You're particularly forward.

Ye've mair gas than a thoosan dummies.
You're far too talkative for my liking.

And finally

Even 1,000 examples merely scratch the surface of the richness of current vernacular in the North-east.

I hope this collection has sparked discussions and fired memories. If so, I'd like to hear examples of words and phrases which have amused you and which you know are in current use.

They don't have to be aul-farrant, as long as they are as colourful and as descriptive as the Doric and the dialect can be.

Please jot them down and send them to me when you have a moment.

Norman Harper
Spik o the Place
Canongate Books Ltd.
14 High Street
Edinburgh
EH1 1TE